Jazz Improvisation for Guitar

A Harmonic Approach

To access audio visit:
www.halleonard.com/mylibrary

"Enter Code"
2571-5767-8933-3219

Garrison Fewell

Edited by Jonathan Feist

Berklee Press

Vice President: David Kusek
Dean of Continuing Education: Debbie Cavalier
Chief Operating Officer: Robert F. Green
Managing Editor: Jonathan Feist
Editorial Assistants: Mina Cho, Yousun Choi, Martin Fowler,
Emily Goldstein, Rajasri Mallikarjuna, Claudia Obser
Cover Designer: Kathy Kikkert
Cover Photo: Luciano Rossetti, © Phocus Agency

Recording Credits

Garrison Fewell, guitar
Dmitry Ishenko, bass
Steve Langone, drums

Recording engineered and mastered by Peter Kontrimas at Pete's Basement Studio, Westwood, Massachusetts.

ISBN 978-0-87639-104-4

1140 Boylston Street
Boston, MA 02215-3693 USA
(617) 747-2146

Visit Berklee Press Online at
www.berkleepress.com

DISTRIBUTED BY

HAL•LEONARD®
7777 W. BLUEMOUND RD. P.O. BOX 13819
MILWAUKEE, WISCONSIN 53213

Visit Hal Leonard Online at
www.halleonard.com

Contents

Audio Tracks

Bold type indicates trio tracks.

Acknowledgments

I offer my sincere thanks to all those who have made valuable contributions to my second book for Berklee Press. Special thanks go to my editor Jonathan Feist for helping organize some of the most difficult chapters (readers will have to figure out which ones those are!) and to Joe Mulholland, chair of the Berklee Harmony Department, for his expert harmonic advice.

I would like to acknowledge my friend and colleague, Alex Ulanowsky, former chair of Berklee's Harmony Department. We worked together as visiting professors at Rotterdam Conservatory in Holland and conducted master classes and lectures throughout Europe with a goal to integrate harmonic analysis and improvisation. Several chapters from this book were developed from those lectures.

My thanks to the many schools and conservatories in Europe who hosted me, sometimes for weeks or months at a time while I worked on this material, especially Masstricht, Amsterdam, Rotterdam, the American School of Modern Music in Paris, Graz, the Freiburg Jazz and Rock School, Cologne, Academia Musica Moderna in Italy, and Leipzig Conservatory where I first presented the chapter on counterpoint and the music of Bach and Charlie Parker.

Thanks to Larry Baione, chair of Berklee's guitar department, and to all my students who have enabled me to practice and perfect my craft every day. A sincere thank you to Martin Fowler, Emily Goldstein, and the other work-study students at Berklee Press who transferred my handwritten music into Finale; to Peter Kontrimas for recording the audio tracks (all ninety-six of them!); and to Steve Langone and Dmitry Ishenko for accompanying me on the trio parts.

I would like to express heartfelt appreciation and gratitude to my mentor, Daisaku Ikeda, for encouraging me to create value as an artist and to develop the courage, wisdom, and compassion to contribute positively to jazz education.

I extend my most sincere thanks to you, the reader, for the opportunity to share my thoughts with you.

Introduction

The purpose of this book is to explore the relationship between jazz harmony and improvisation by studying the *vertical* structures of chords and their function in a progression, and the *horizontal* or linear application of harmony to melodic improvisation. Each topic is accompanied by musical examples that are designed to help you hear the connection between harmony and melody and develop a more melodic and creative way of thinking about improvising over chord progressions.

The basic elements that contribute to any good improvised solo are melody, rhythm, and harmony. Depending on the player and the intent of the moment, any one of these could predominate, and the balance may naturally change during the course of a solo.

Harmonic improvisation, on an instrument like guitar, emphasizes the use of vertical extensions on individual chords and the overall tonal structure of a progression, while *melodic* improvisation emphasizes single-note lines with distinctive melodic contour and a strong sense of rhythm that flow through a series of chords.

Frequently considered "horn-like" in nature, melodic improvisation can be applied to guitar where the effect of playing single-note lines like a saxophone is enhanced by the use of articulations such as glissandos, pull-offs, slurs, and rest-stroke picking (a.k.a. sweep picking) in the right hand. Guitarists Jim Hall and Grant Green have been associated with this style. Hall claims Charlie Christian, Django Reinhardt, and saxophonists Ben Webster and Jimmy Giuffre as having contributed to his melodic approach. Green cited Miles Davis and a little bit of Charlie Parker as his primary influences.

Melodic playing reflects harmony but is not necessarily controlled by it. Sometimes you'll hear the chord changes in an improvised solo, and other times the melody seems to float above the harmony like a cloud that casts a fleeting shadow over the ground.

Simply knowing the right tensions on a chord or which scales to play over a certain progression does not ensure the creation of a memorable solo. A more musical approach is to extract melodic material from within the scales.

And there are many examples of brilliant improvisers who played the "wrong" notes in some of the best solos ever recorded.

So which notes are the right "wrong" notes? And what do really good players think of while improvising? Are they connecting scales? Are they thinking about the arpeggios of each chord? Do they automatically know the tensions on every chord? How can you look at a piece of music, interpret the harmonic variations, and know what to play? How can guitarists put all these things together and quickly visualize them on the fretboard?

This book attempts to answer those questions . . . and more.

The ability to negotiate the changes in a tune, play substitutions, and weave triads and arpeggios into a smoothly crafted solo, to form combinations of melodic and rhythmic motifs into coherent lines, to choose the right colors that reflect the harmonic and emotional content of a composition—these are important talents a jazz guitarist should aspire to develop.

What You Need to Know

This book is suited to guitarists who are seeking to improve their ability to understand jazz harmony and improvise over chord changes. To feel comfortable working with the materials presented in this book, you should have some familiarity with key signatures, major and minor scales, intervals, triads, seventh chords, diatonic harmony, and chord progressions. A basic understanding of jazz phrasing and rhythm will help you derive maximum benefit from the exercises you will be playing.

How to Practice

In order to improve your technique, play along with the melodic examples on the audio, paying close attention to articulation and rhythm. Fingerings are included with all examples and TAB notation indicates suggested positions on the fretboard. Memorize the melodic phrases and practice transposing them to other keys, working out alternate fingerings as you move through various positions on the guitar.

At the end of each chapter, you will find either an etude or a practice progression with rhythm section accompaniment where you can try out melodic phrases and apply the knowledge you have learned by inventing your own solos.

Learning tunes by listening to recordings of great players who have contributed to the legacy of jazz is highly recommended and suggested examples are included at various points throughout the book.

Resources for studying harmony and improvisation extend beyond jazz compositions. In the last two chapters, I cite examples of melodic counterpoint by the most inventive melodist ever, J.S. Bach, while demonstrating comparisons with improvisations by saxophonist Charlie Parker. In the conclusion of this book, you will learn how to build solos with chromatic motion and compound lines using the principles of classical counterpoint.

CHAPTER I

Diatonic Substitution and Upper-Structure Triads

Triad substitution is the use of triads derived from the chord tones and melodic extensions of a chord, beyond the basic triad. These triads can be categorized as either *diatonic substitutions* (triads that only contain chord degrees 1, 3, 5, 6, or 7) or *upper-structure triads* (triads that contain at least one tension). Drawing notes from these triads highlights additional colors in your improvising.

To find the extensions of a CMaj7 chord, start from the root and move upward by alternating intervals of major and minor thirds. This gives you tensions 9, ♯11, and 13, which spells a D major triad.

Note that the 11th degree is raised in this example, to become ♯11. This usually occurs in the Lydian mode but can be effectively used on any major 7 chord, and it offers more triads for building phrases than the natural 11.

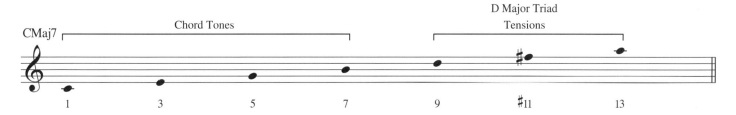

Fig. 1.1 Chord Tones and Tensions of CMaj7

Figure 1.2 illustrates the sequential triad extensions of CMaj7. The E– and A– triads are diatonic substitutions for CMaj7. They are both tonic chords (III– and VI–) in the key of C and contain chord tones 1, 3, 5, 6, and 7 of CMaj7. The G, B–, and D triads are upper-structure triads containing tensions 9 and ♯11 of CMaj7.

The F♯° triad is a very unstable sound on CMaj7 and is not used as often as the other triads.

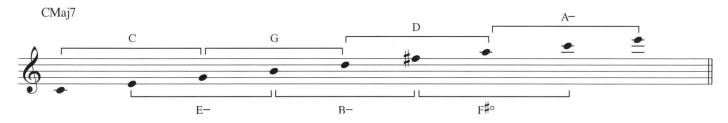

Fig. 1.2. Diatonic and Upper-Structure Triad Substitutions for CMaj7

Building Phrases Using Triad Substitutions

The phrase in figure 1.3 uses a combination of E–, A–, and G triads. The triads are bracketed to help you see the shapes on the fretboard.

Track 1

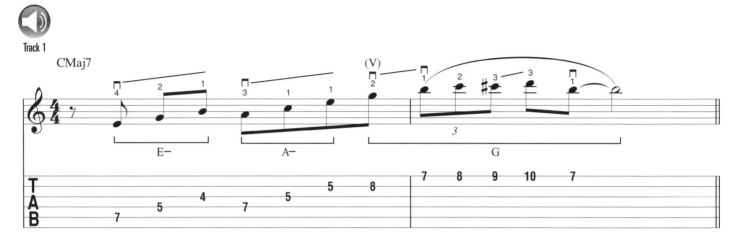

Fig. 1.3. Melodic Phrase Using Triad Substitutions

Tip: Right-Hand Technique

It is important to work on the right-hand technique for this phrase (figure 1.3), using a rest stroke attack (indicated by the ⊓——). If you play this phrase with your thumb, like Wes Montgomery, it feels very natural to play all downstrokes. Don't take your thumb off the strings between notes; just keep the pressure on from string to string as you move across the neck. Rest strokes add a rhythmic "pop" to the lines, and make it easier to play this phrase at fast tempos.

When using a pick in the right hand, adjust the pressure to resemble the way it feels with your thumb. Remember not to lift up the pick when moving from string to string in the middle of a rest stroke, and increase the speed gradually until you can play it smoothly.

One alternative is to play an upstroke on the last note of the first measure (indicated by the V).

Now transpose this phrase and play it over Maj7 chords in other keys. The following example leads you through the keys of C, E♭, A♭, and D♭. Notice that you will use a different fingering for the phrase on the A♭Maj7 chord, but you can keep the same rest-stroke approach in the right hand.

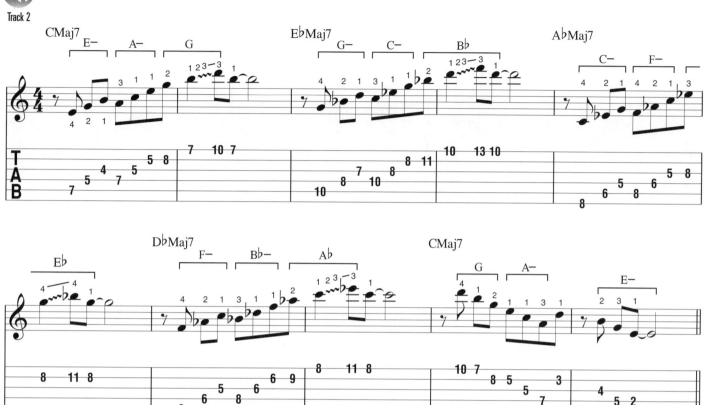

Fig. 1.4. Triad Substitutions over CMaj7, EbMaj7, AbMaj7, and DbMaj7 Chords

In order to learn the triads over Maj7 chords in all keys, transpose this progression up a perfect 4th to the key of F Major. Notice how the patterns shift to other positions on the neck while using the same two fingerings.

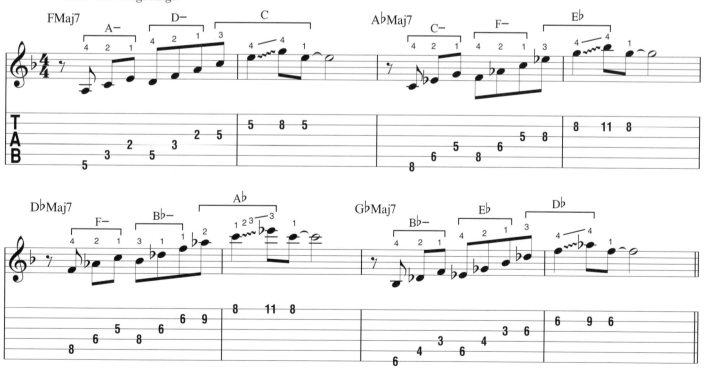

Fig. 1.5. Triad Substitutions over Progression in F Major

You can keep moving the progression through the cycle of fifths, practicing these lines in all keys. The next transposition would be: BbMaj7 / DbMaj7 / GbMaj7 / BMaj7.

Upper-Structure Triads

The upper-structure triads for CMaj7 are G, D, and B– (see figure 1.2). Together, these triads contain the 7th, 9th, ♯11th, and 13th degrees of CMaj7.

Figure 1.6 illustrates a B– triad played over CMaj7.

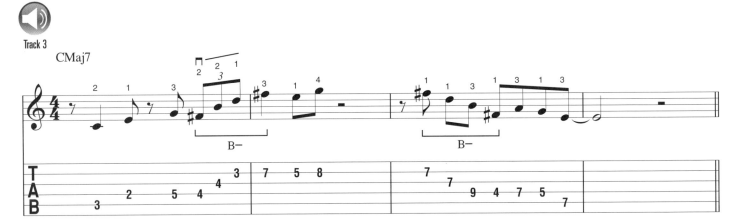

Fig. 1.6. B– Upper-Structure Triad Used over CMaj7 Chord

Polyrhythms

When a continuous series of triads is played in 4/4 time, it creates a polyrhythmic feel of 3/4 against the basic 4/4 meter. When you repeat a series of triads one after the other, the resulting three-note pattern makes it feel like the pulse or rhythmic accent shifts. This is a useful rhythmic approach that works with all diatonic and upper-structure triads.

The melodic example in figure 1.7 uses a combination of diatonic and upper-structure triads over CMaj7 (B–, E–, D, and G).

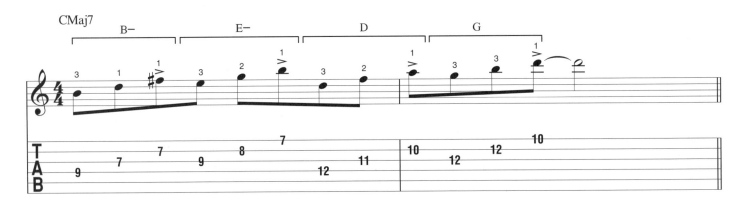

Fig. 1.7. Polyrhythmic Effect

Rhythmic Displacement

The phrase in figure 1.7 can be started at any point in the measure: on the first beat, on the "and" of beat 1, or on the "and" of beat 4 in the previous bar. This "rhythmic displacement" of the melodic phrase shifts the polyrhythmic accents.

Here is the same phrase starting on the "and" of 1.

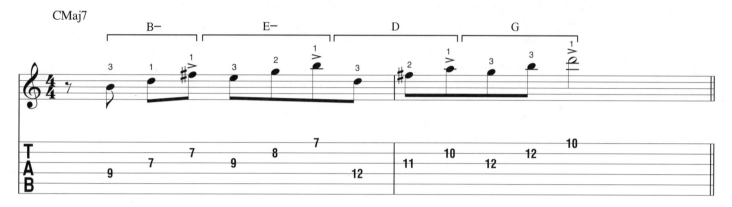

Fig. 1.8. Rhythmic Displacement. Phrase begins on the "and" of beat 1.

In figure 1.9, the phrase starts on the "and" of beat 4, anticipating the first measure.

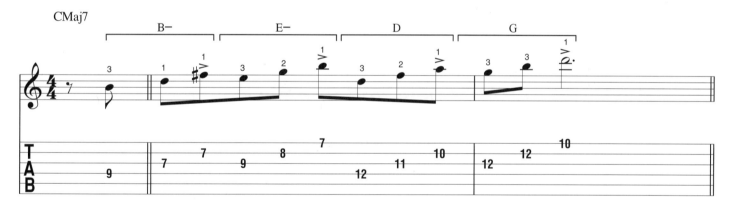

Fig. 1.9. Phrase Begins on the "and" of Beat 4

Figure 1.10 is a melodic example of diatonic and upper-structure triads over CMaj7: E–, D, A–, and B–. Listen to the effect of rhythmic displacement in this phrase. It starts on beat 1 and then repeats starting on the "and" of beat 1 in bar 4.

Track 4

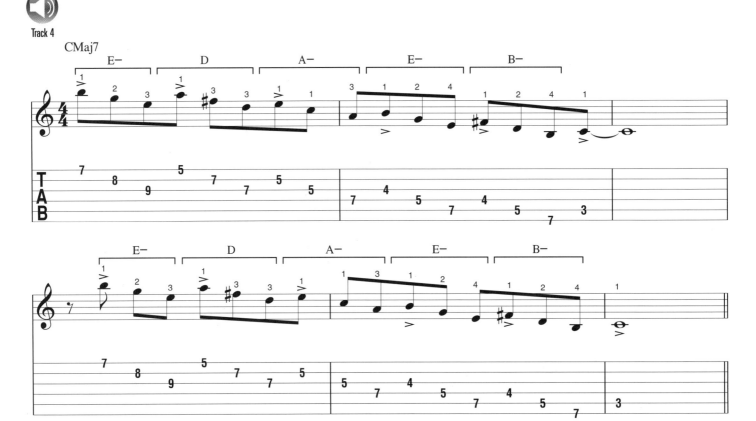

Fig. 1.10. Rhythmic Displacement

Rhythmic Displacement within a Phrase

Another type of rhythmic displacement is the use of rests and varied rhythm to create unusual or unexpected phrasing from triads. There are only two triads at work in this next phrase: E– and D, but the use of rhythmic displacement illustrates multiple possibilities. Listen carefully to how the triads are displaced by the triplet rhythm in measures 3 and 4.

Track 5

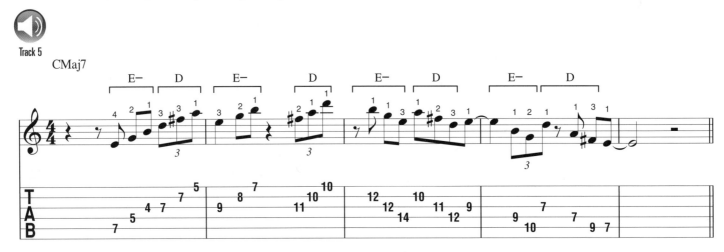

Fig. 1.11. Rhythmic Displacement within Phrases

Triad Substitution over a II–7 / V7 / I Progression

Triads can also be used to play melodic phrases over a II–7 / V7 / I progression. The sound of the triads and the tensions on each individual chord becomes less important than the overall shape of the phrase and the continuity of the line moving up and down the fretboard.

Figures 1.12 and 1.13 are two examples:

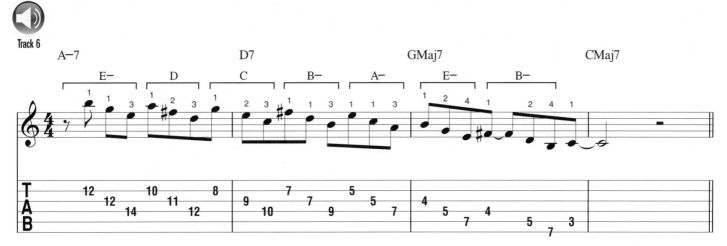

Fig. 1.12. Triads over a II–7 / V7 / I Progression in G

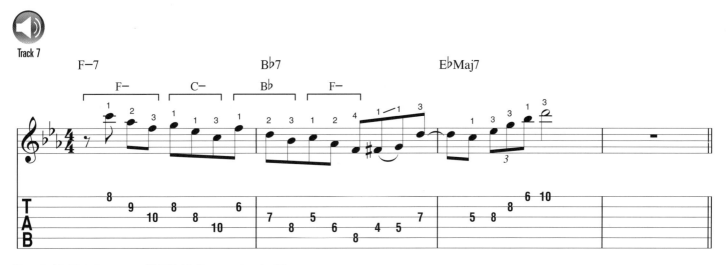

Fig. 1.13. Triads over a II / V / I Progression in E♭

Etude

The following etude uses the techniques discussed in this chapter, particularly diatonic and upper-structure triad substitution, over a II / V / I / VI progression through a cycle of fourths. On the audio, you will hear the first sixteen bars.

ETUDE

Track 8

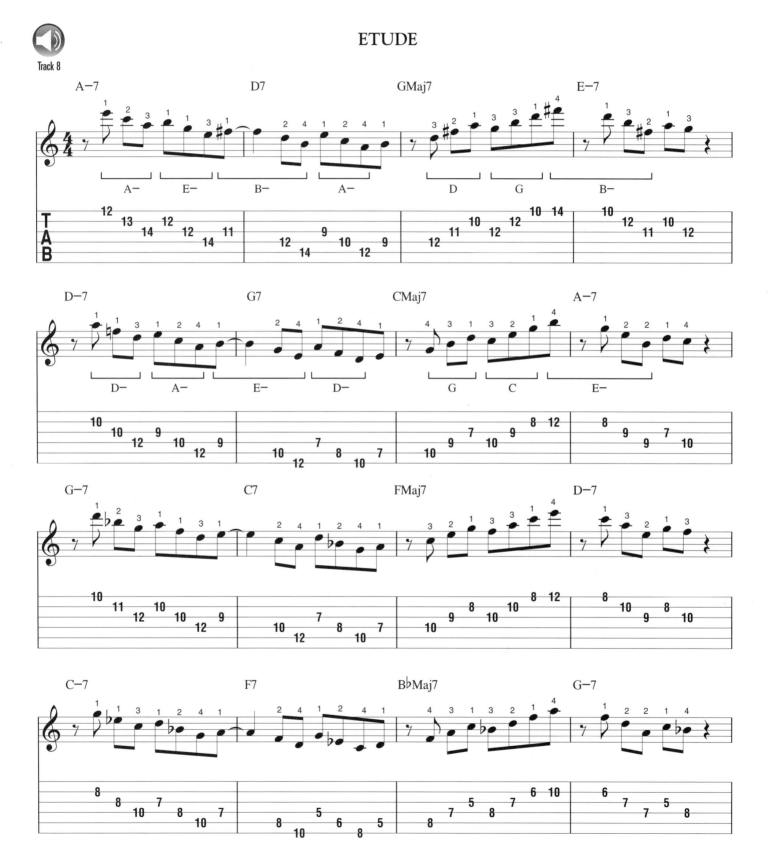

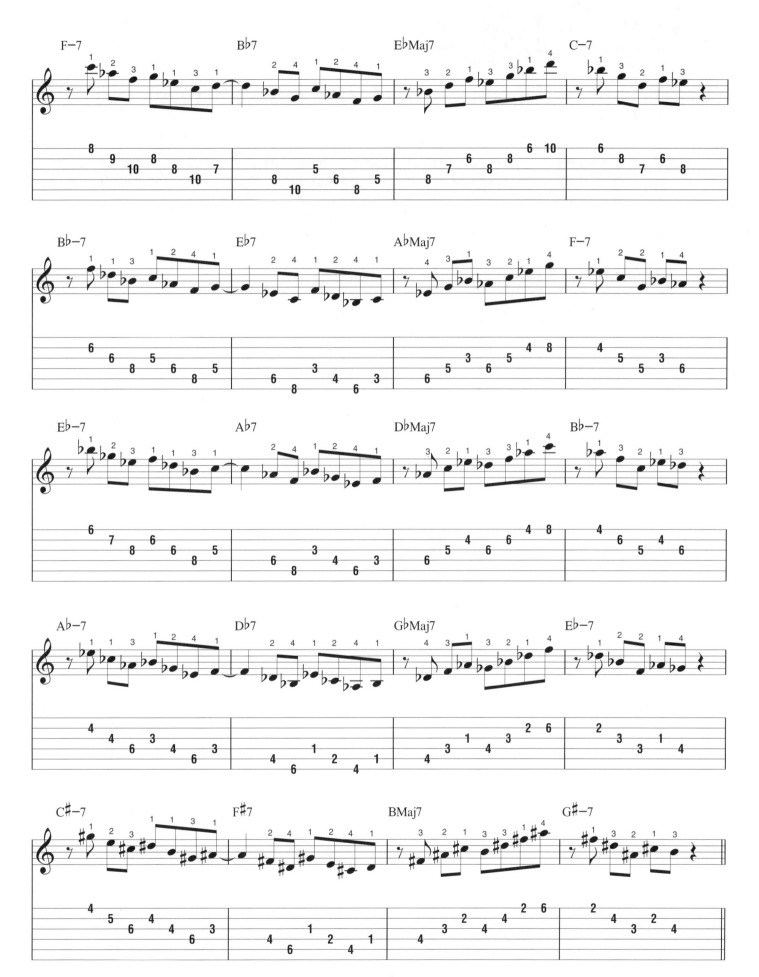

Fig. 1.14. Triads over II / V / I / VI Progression in Cycle of Fourths

CHAPTER 2

Diatonic Substitution: 7th Chord Arpeggios

Similar to diatonic and upper-structure triads, *diatonic 7th chord substitutions* also come from the extensions of a chord by moving upward from the root in intervals of diatonic thirds. The resulting 4-note arpeggios can be played as *melodic substitutions* over the original chord. Because they contain the available tensions of the original chord, these substitutions allow you to highlight different areas of color when improvising.

Arpeggio Substitutions for CMaj7

Figure 2.1 shows how 7th chord arpeggio substitutions are derived from the extensions of a CMaj7 chord. Tension ♯11 (F♯) is an available tension in the C Lydian mode and adds more possible substitutions for improvising over Maj7 chords. The most common arpeggio substitutions for CMaj7 are E–7, GMaj7, and B–7.

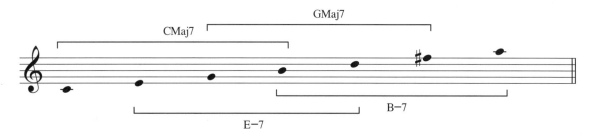

Fig. 2.1. CMaj7 and Possible Arpeggio Substitutions

E–7 (III–7) is a diatonic substitution for CMaj7 (IMaj7). E–7 contains the 3rd, 5th, 7th, and 9th of CMaj7.

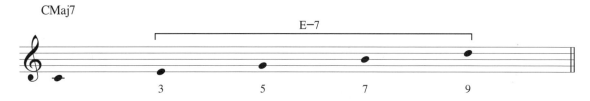

Fig. 2.2. E–7 as a Substitute for CMaj7

Figure 2.3 is a melodic phrase that demonstrates an E–7 arpeggio substitution over a CMaj7 chord. There are three different fingerings for the same line so that you can play it in any position on the neck. This is helpful when you transpose to other keys.

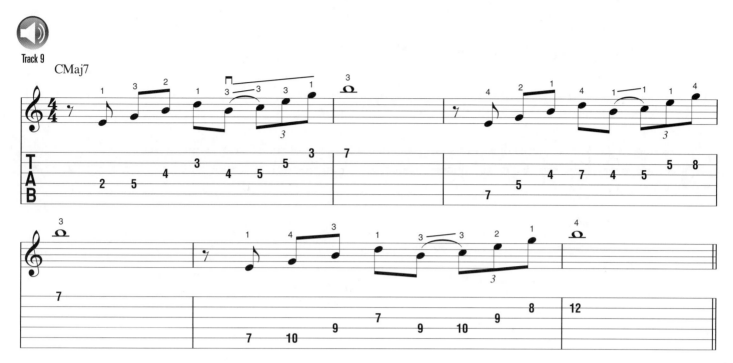

Track 9

Fig. 2.3. Melodic Line Substituting E–7 for CMaj7

GMaj7 and B–7 Arpeggio Substitutions for CMaj7

GMaj7 and B–7 arpeggios contain the 5th, 7th, 9th, ♯11th, and 13th degrees of CMaj7. These substitutions highlight the extensions of CMaj7 and have a very transparent or "cool" sound because they don't contain the root or major third degree of CMaj7. They tend to disguise the sound of CMaj7 and are therefore called *hybrid substitutions* (explained in more detail later in this chapter).

Figure 2.4 analyzes GMaj7 and B–7 arpeggios in relation to their function over CMaj7(♯11).

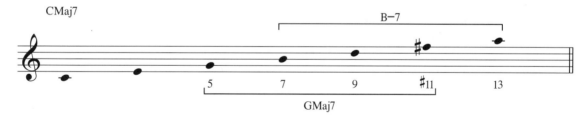

Fig. 2.4. GMaj7 and B–7 Arpeggio Substitutions for CMaj7

Figure 2.5 is a melodic example using three combinations of 7th chord substitutions over CMaj7: E–7 / B–7 / GMaj7.

Track 10

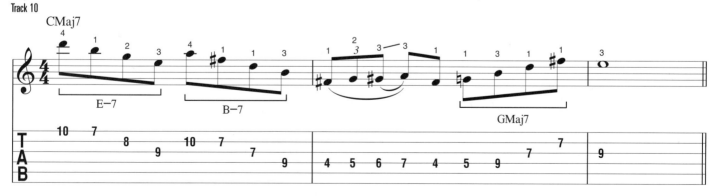

Fig. 2.5. Melodic Line Substituting E–7, B–7, and GMaj7 for CMaj7

Direct and Indirect Melodic Resolution

The #11 always sounds good on a major 7 chord, especially when you consider the #11 as a chromatic approach to the 5th degree of the major 7 chord.

Figure 2.6 is an example of a GMaj7 arpeggio over CMaj7 with the #11 (F#) as a chromatic approach to the 5th (G) using direct and indirect melodic resolution.

Track 11

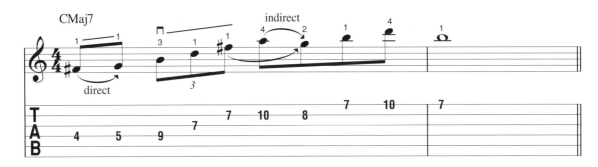

Fig. 2.6. GMaj7 Arpeggio Substitution for CMaj7 with F# as an Approach Note to G

And for the nimble-fingered fretmaster who likes to cover multiple positions in a single phrase, try this extension of the previous line. It sounds great when played as a cadenza at the end of a tune where tensions 9 and #11 add a brighter color to the CMaj7 chord.

Track 12

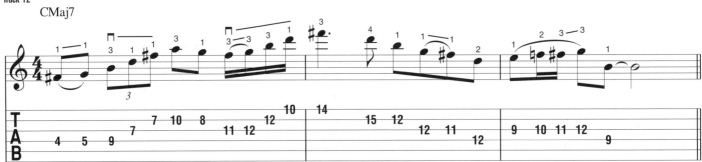

Fig. 2.7. GMaj7 Substitution Variation (Multiple Positions)

#IV–7♭5 Arpeggio Substitution for CMaj7

An F#–7♭5 (#IV–7♭5) arpeggio contains the #11th, 6th, root, and 3rd degrees of CMaj7 (IMaj7).

Fig. 2.8. F#–7♭5 as a Substitute for CMaj7

The following example is a melodic line that demonstrates an F#–7♭5 arpeggio over CMaj7. The beginning of the first measure contains an indirect chromatic approach used in bebop phrases: C#, B, to C.

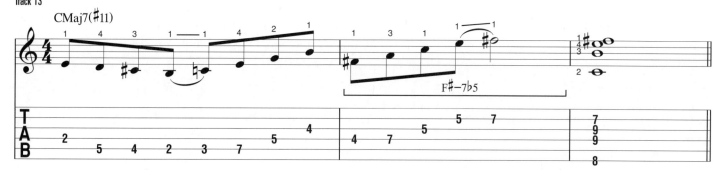

Fig. 2.9. Melodic Line with F#–7♭5 Substitute for CMaj7

Quick Tip to Find Arpeggio Substitutions for a Maj7 Chord

1. Play a minor 7th arpeggio starting on the 3rd degree of a major 7 chord (E–7/CMaj7).

2. Play a major 7 arpeggio starting from the 5th degree of a major 7 chord (GMaj7/CMaj7).

3. Play a minor 7 arpeggio starting from the 7th degree of a major 7 chord (B–7/CMaj7).

4. Play a minor 7♭5 arpeggio starting from the #4th degree of a major 7 chord (F#–7♭5/CMaj7).

Arpeggio Substitutions for Minor 7 Chords

When A–7 is VI–7 in the key of C, the diatonic extensions include the other tonic chords in the key of C: E–7 and CMaj7. These substitutions contain tensions 9 (B) and 11 (D) on the A–7 chord.

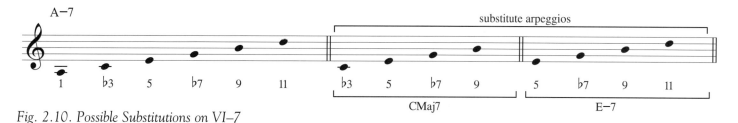

Fig. 2.10. Possible Substitutions on VI–7

Here is a melodic example of diatonic substitution (E–7 and CMaj7 arpeggios) over an A–7 chord.

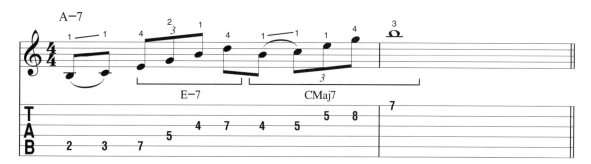

Fig. 2.11. Melodic Phrase with E–7 and CMaj7 Substituting for A–7

E–7 and CMaj7 arpeggios also work as melodic substitutions when A–7 is a tonic chord (I–7).

For the Flying Fret Brothers Club (related to the Wright Brothers, masters of flight) here is one more line. Look carefully, because it's similar to the previous example, only it spans the 2nd to the 12th frets and shifts positions in the middle of the line without stopping to refuel in mid-flight.

Track 14

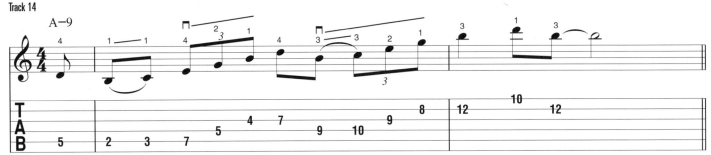

Fig. 2.12. *VI–7 Substitution Variation across Multiple Frets*

Arpeggio Substitutions for Dominant 7 Chords

Diatonic substitution can be applied to V7 chords in a similar way as the previous examples.

G7 is the V7 chord in the key of C. Start with the notes in a G7 chord and extend upwards by intervals of diatonic thirds.

The first substitute is B–7♭5 (B, D, F, A) and adds tension 9 to the G7 chord.

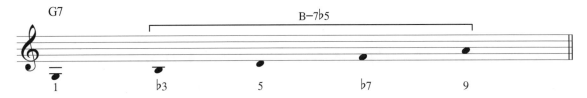

Fig. 2.13. *VII–7♭5 as a Substitution for V7*

Playing a minor 7♭5 arpeggio from the 3rd degree of a V7 chord is a simple and efficient way to build phrases on a II–7 / V7 / I progression.

Here is an example for D–7 / G7 / CMaj7 that uses arpeggio substitutes FMaj7 over D–7 and B–7♭5 for G7 and transposes the line to B♭–7 / E♭7 / A♭Maj7. With these two fingerings you'll be able to play the line in all keys.

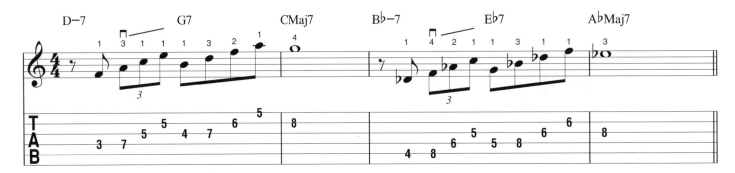

Fig. 2.14. *Melodic Phrases with Substitutions for G7*

Melodic Substitution Using Hybrids

You have learned how playing diatonic 7th chord arpeggios as melodic substitutions allows you to highlight different areas of color within a chord. In addition to diatonic substitution and upper-structure triads, hybrids are another important type of substitution.

Hybrid Voicings

A *hybrid voicing* is one where the upper-structure triad or chord does not contain either the root or third degree of the original chord. Hybrids are most often found in reharmonization of chords using triads over a bass note ("slash chords"). Because the upper structure doesn't contain the root or third of the original chord, it creates a more ambiguous sound, which is characteristic of contemporary jazz.

For example, if the original chord is CMaj7, you might play a hybrid voicing (a triad over a bass note) such as G/C (this implies a CMaj7[9]). Other choices are D/C and B–/C (where the F♯ implies a CMaj7[♯11]). The G, D, and B– triads are hybrids because they don't contain the root (C) or third (E) of CMaj7.

Another very common hybrid voicing, B♭/C, is used for C9sus4.

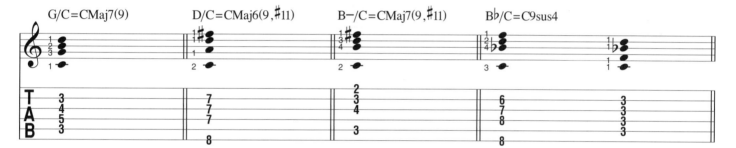

Fig. 2.15. *Hybrid Voicings: Triads over a Bass Note*

Hybrid Substitution with 7th Chord Arpeggios

You can also use 7th chords as hybrids if they don't contain the root or 3rd degree of the original chord. Earlier in this chapter you played GMaj7 and B–7 arpeggios over CMaj7 (figure 2.4). GMaj7/C and B–7/C are hybrids for CMaj7 precisely because they don't contain the root or 3rd degree of CMaj7. Improvising with hybrid arpeggio substitutions creates a transparent, or "modern" sound, especially evident when there is no harmonic accompaniment—just the sound of a hybrid arpeggio played over a bass note. (You can hear something like this on Pat Metheny's recording, *Bright Size Life*).

Dominant 7sus4 and Hybrid Substitute Arpeggios

The dominant 7sus4 chord is one of the most common sounds in contemporary music, playing a prominent role in the "modal style" of compositions such as McCoy Tyner's "Passion Dance," Wayne Shorter's "House of Jade" and "Night Dreamer," Herbie Hancock's "Maiden Voyage," and Miles Davis's "Eighty-One." The common denominator in those tunes is that they all feature modal sections with various unrelated dominant 7sus4 chords. Standards such as "The Night Has a Thousand Eyes" and Horace Silver's "Moon Rays" also feature the V7sus4 chord.

The most common hybrid substitute for V7sus4 is to play a minor 7 arpeggio starting from the 5th degree of the sus4 chord. In other words, play a D–7 arpeggio over G7sus4. This adds tensions 9 and 11 to the G7 chord.

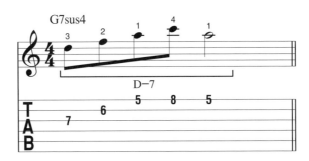

Fig. 2.16. D–7 as a Hybrid Substitute for G7sus4

An FMaj7 substitution adds tensions 9 and 13 to the G7 chord so that it becomes G7sus4 (9,13).

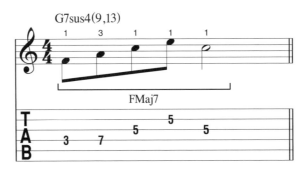

Fig. 2.17. FMaj7 as a Hybrid Substitute for G7sus4

Here are some examples of lines using arpeggios D–7 and FMaj7 to play over G7sus4. In each example, a chord voicing is used as a reference point for playing the phrase. You'll notice that the contour of the line fits closely to the shape of the chord and the area of the fretboard where the voicing is played.

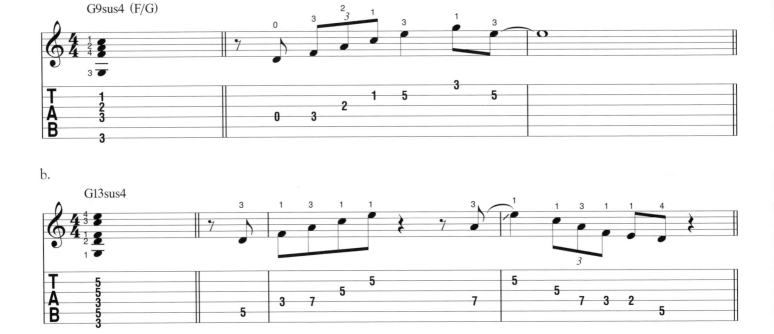

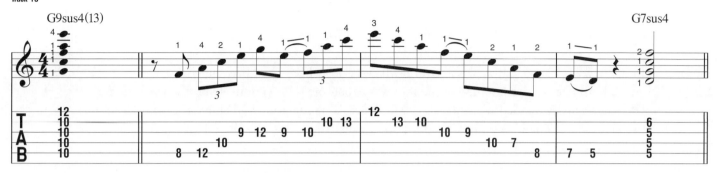

Fig. 2.18. Melodic Phrases Using Substitutions for G7sus4 Chords

Reharmonization of Melodies Using Diatonic, Hybrid, and Polychords

Until this point, you have used melodic substitution to accent different chord tones and tensions within a single chord structure. You can expand this idea further by playing the *same* melody with *different* harmonies (*reharmonization*). The sound of each chord impacts the melodic phrase according to the relationship between melody and harmony.

In the following example, an EbMaj7 chord and its melodic extensions reveal four separate 4-note structures: EbMaj7 (original chord sound), G–7 (diatonic substitution), BbMaj7 (hybrid), and D–7 (hybrid).

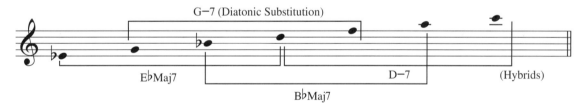

Fig. 2.19. EbMaj7 and Melodic Extensions

The EbMaj7 and G–7 arpeggios can be combined to make one melody.

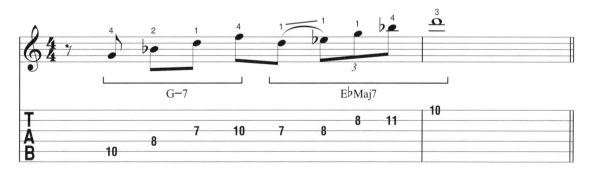

Fig. 2.20. Melody with Combination of G–7 and EbMaj7 Arpeggios

Using *reharmonization*, you can play this melody over different chords. And over each chord, you get different sounds with more or less tension depending on what chords you're playing on. Instead of playing a different melodic line for every chord change, playing the same melody over different chords enables you to become more efficient in your use of vocabulary.

In figure 2.21, the melody is played over E♭Maj7, C–7, A♭Maj7, and F7sus4. The arpeggios (G–7 and E♭Maj7) are analyzed to determine if they are diatonic substitutions, hybrids, or polychords. (*Polychords* are two independent triads or 7th chords, one superimposed above the other, where both can sound simultaneously.) The tensions are circled to illustrate the relative density of upper-structure sounds over each chord.

Track 16

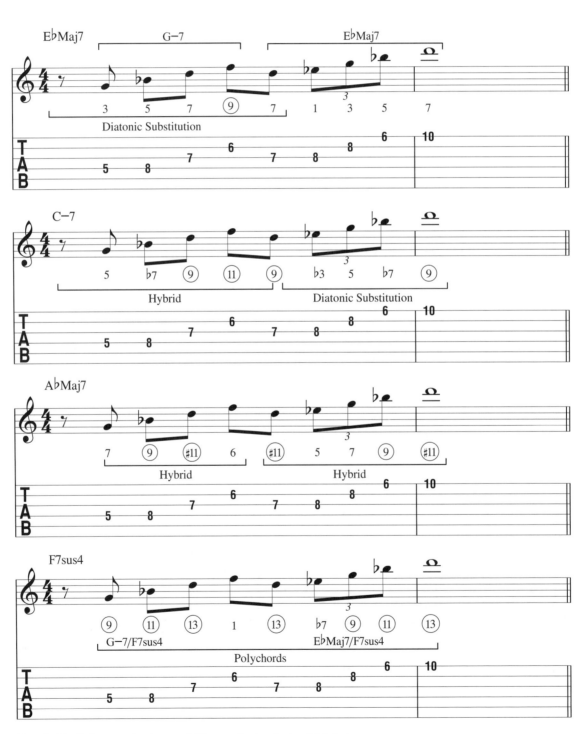

Fig. 2.21. Reharmonization and Harmonic Analysis of Melody

From the melodic extensions of E♭Maj7 (Figure 2.22), two more arpeggios (B♭Maj7 and D–7) can be combined to play a similar melodic line.

Fig.2.22. Melody with Combination of D–7 and B♭Maj7 arpeggios

In the following example, the melody is played over E♭Maj7, G–7, B♭Maj7, and C7sus4. The B♭Maj7 and D–7 arpeggios are analyzed on each chord to determine if they are diatonic substitutions, hybrids, or polychords.

Track 17

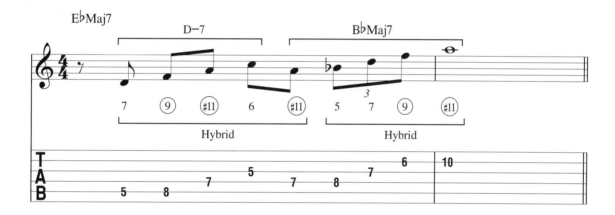

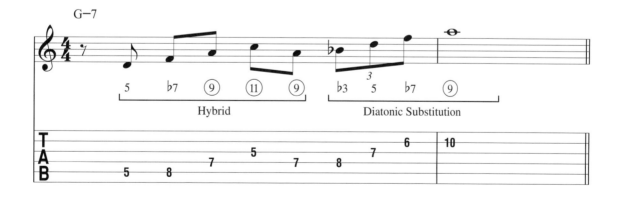

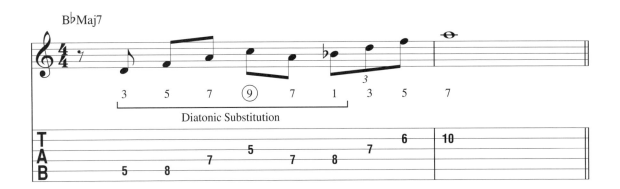

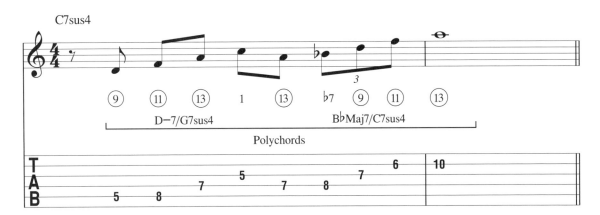

Fig. 2.23. *Reharmonization of Melody with Harmonic Analysis*

Here is a reference chart summarizing the previous examples of melodic reharmonization using diatonic, hybrid, and polychords. In the left column, G–7 and E♭Maj7 arpeggios are analyzed over E♭Maj7, C–7, A♭Maj7, and F7sus4. In the right column, D–7 and B♭Maj7 arpeggios are analyzed over E♭Maj7, G–7, B♭Maj7, and C7sus4.

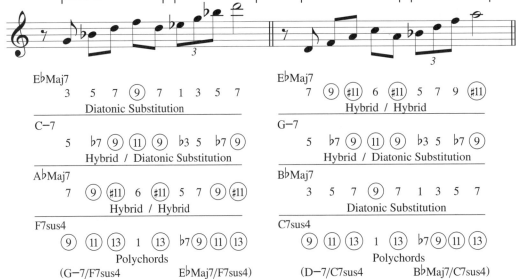

Fig. 2.24. *Melodic Reharmonization Using Diatonic, Hybrid, and Polychords*

A THOUSAND NIGHTS

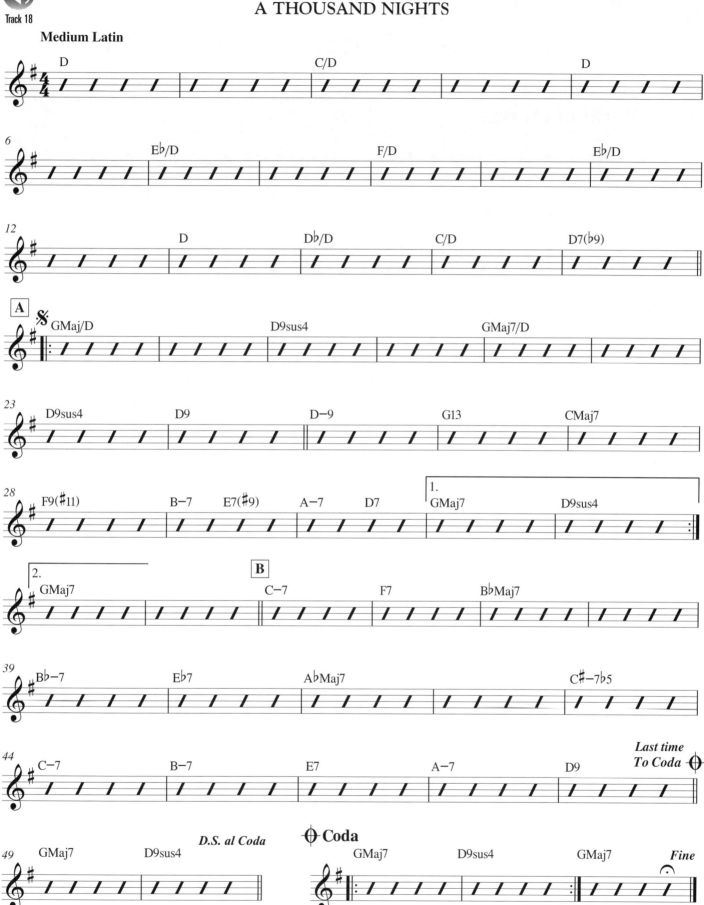

Fig. 2.25. "A Thousand Nights" (Trio Track)

CHAPTER 3
Parallel Modes and Diatonic Substitution

Parallel Modes

Parallel modes are different modes or scales starting on the same tonic. For example, C Aeolian, C Dorian, and C Phrygian are parallel modes because they all start on the note C. Scales such as C major, C melodic minor, C harmonic minor, and C natural minor are also considered parallel modes because they start on the same tonic.

Chord progressions with parallel modes appear frequently in standard tunes. In this chapter, you will learn how to put the power of parallel modes to work when improvising over chord changes, learn how to use diatonic substitution in minor keys, and play solos with more harmonic depth.

Songs often change from one mode to another while the basic tonal center remains the same. The use of parallel modes in short sections (several measures) is referred to as *modal interchange*, meaning the interchangeability of different modes based on the same tonic. The use of parallel modes in longer song sections is referred to as *pan modality*. Because most tunes don't stay in just one mode, you need to know all the chords for each mode so that you will recognize the movement from one mode to another, as the change may be subtle and happen frequently. It is not uncommon to find four different modes in four measures, one after the next.

The first step to understanding parallel modes is to learn the diatonic chords from each of the four principal "parent" scales in the key of C: C major, C natural minor, C melodic minor, and C harmonic minor.

C Major

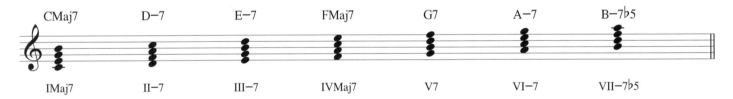

C Natural Minor

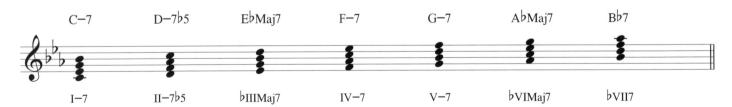

C Melodic Minor

C–(Maj7)	D–7	E♭Maj7♯5	F7	G7	A–7♭5	B–7♭5
I–(Maj7)	II–7	♭IIIMaj7♯5	IV7	V7	VI–7♭5	VII–7♭5

C Harmonic Minor

C–(Maj7)	D–7♭5	E♭Maj7♯5	F–7	G7	A♭Maj7	B°7
I–(Maj7)	II–7♭5	♭IIIMaj7♯5	IV–7	V7	♭VIMaj7	VII°7

Fig. 3.1. Diatonic Chords for the Four Principal Parent Scales Starting on C

Diatonic Chord Progressions

The next step is to identify typical diatonic chord progressions in each mode, and to memorize the tensions (or "color tones") on the V7 chord in each mode. Just remember that tensions on the V7 chord come from the diatonic notes of the "parent" scale or tonality to which the V7 chord belongs, whether it's derived from major, natural minor, melodic minor, or harmonic minor.

Major: The most common chord progression in a major tonality is IMaj7 / VI–7 / II–7 / V7 (CMaj7 / A–7 / D–7 / G7 in the key of C major). The tensions on the V7 chord in a major key are 9 and 13.

Compositions such as "I'm Old Fashioned," "Polkadots and Moonbeams," "The Way You Look Tonight," "Long Ago and Far Away," "Emily," "Time After Time," "My Heart Stood Still" and "I've Never Been in Love Before" employ the I / VI / II / V progression.

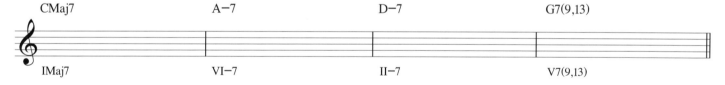

Fig. 3.2. I / VI / II / V Progression in C Major

Melodic Minor: The I / VI / II / V progression when transposed to melodic minor becomes I–6 / VI–7♭5 / II–7 / V7 (9, ♭13). Tensions on the V7 chord in melodic minor are 9 and ♭13.

Jazz compositions often feature I–6 or I–(Maj7) chords from the melodic minor scale. Horace Silver's "Nica's Dream" begins with a Min(Maj7) chord, while bossa novas such as "Corcovado" and "Gentle Rain" start on a tonic Min6 chord. More common are songs that use a combination of chords from different modes (modal interchange) such as "Yesterdays," "'Round Midnight," and "Minority."

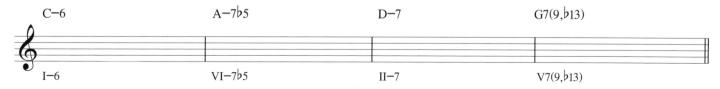

Fig. 3.3. I–6 / VI–7♭5 / II–7 / V7 (9,♭13) Progression in C Melodic Minor

Harmonic Minor: Transposed to the harmonic minor scale, the previous progression becomes I–(Maj7) / ♭VIMaj7 / II–7♭5 / V7 (♭9, ♭13). In the key of C harmonic minor: C–(Maj7) / A♭Maj7 / D–7♭5 / G7(♭9). In harmonic minor, tensions on the V7 chord are ♭9 and ♭13.

The II–7♭5 / V7(♭9) progression is an important part of most standard tunes in minor keys: "Autumn Leaves," "Beautiful Love," "Alone Together," and "Black Orpheus" are good examples.

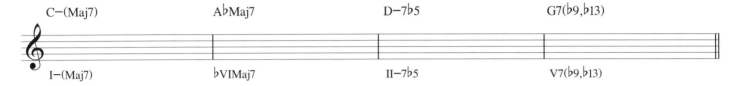

Fig. 3.4. I–(Maj7) / ♭VIMaj7 / II–7♭5 / V7 (♭9,♭13) Progression in C Harmonic Minor

Natural Minor Scale: The natural minor scale doesn't have a V7 chord, but the ♭VII7 chord functions as a dominant chord that resolves up a whole step to the I– chord. A typical progression is I–7 / ♭VIMaj7 / IV–7 / ♭VII7. In the key of C natural minor: C–7 / A♭Maj7 / F–9 / B♭7 (9,13).

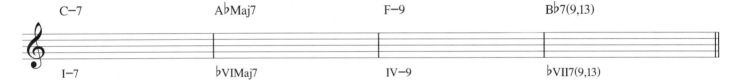

Fig. 3.5. I–7 / ♭VIMaj7 / IV–7 / ♭VII7 Progression in C Natural Minor

One of my favorite jazz compositions featuring the natural minor scale (or Aeolian mode) is Kenny Barron's "Sunshower." The A section alternates between A–7 (I–7) and FMaj7 (♭VIMaj7).

Another progression borrowed from the natural minor scale is IV–7 / ♭VII7, which is frequently used as a modal interchange cadence in major tunes, such as "You Go to My Head."

Improvisation Using Parallel Modes

A good example of parallel modes is the first four bars of "My Funny Valentine." The chords are C– / C–(Maj7) / C–7 / C–6. This progression contains three parallel modes in the key of C minor: C natural minor, C harmonic minor, and C melodic minor.

Below is an analysis of this 4-bar progression with the relative scales you could play over each chord. This progression is called a "descending minor line cliché," because of the chromatic line that starts on the root of the I– chord and moves downward. This results in a *composite minor* progression, because it uses natural, harmonic, and melodic minor scales. It is found in many standards such as "In a Sentimental Mood," "In Walked Bud," "God Bless the Child," and popular tunes such as the Beatles' "Michelle" and Led Zeppelin's "Stairway to Heaven." The chromatic line in figure 3.6 can be used to play a solo that outlines the chord changes.

Fig. 3.6. Opening Chords for "My Funny Valentine." C Minor Line Cliché.

Playing Diatonic Arpeggio Substitutions over Chords

You can play arpeggio substitutions for each chord in the minor line cliché by analyzing the diatonic extensions of each chord.

There are two obvious choices for substitutions to play over C minor: E♭Maj7 and G–7. Beyond the notes of the C– triad, an E♭Maj7 arpeggio adds ♭7 and tension 9, while the G–7 arpeggio adds extensions ♭7, 9, and 11.

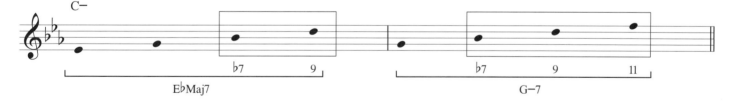

Fig. 3.7. Possible Diatonic Substitutions for C–

Here is a melodic phrase using both G–7 and E♭Maj7 arpeggios over C minor:

Track 19

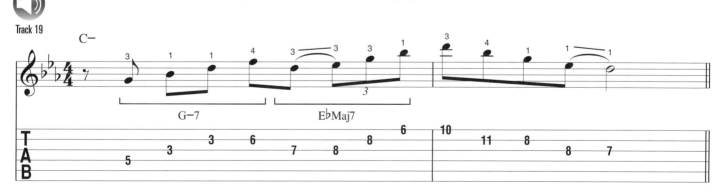

Fig. 3.8. Melodic Phrase with Diatonic Substitutions for C–

In the second measure of the minor line cliché, C–(Maj7) is I–(Maj7) from the C harmonic minor scale. The substitute arpeggios are E♭Maj7♯5 (♭IIIMaj7♯5), which includes the Maj7 and 9th degrees, and G7 (V7), which contains the Maj7, 9th and 11th degrees of C–(Maj7).

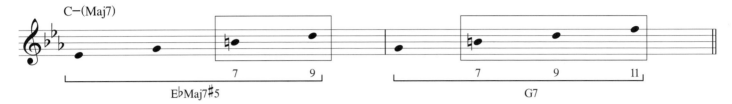

Fig. 3.9. Available Arpeggio Substitutions for C–(Maj7)

Figure 3.10 shows a melodic phrase using E♭Maj7♯5 and G7 arpeggios over C–(Maj7). To get the right feel for this line, use rest-stroke picking on beat 4 of the first measure, and a reverse rest stroke on beat 2 of the second measure (as indicated).

Track 20

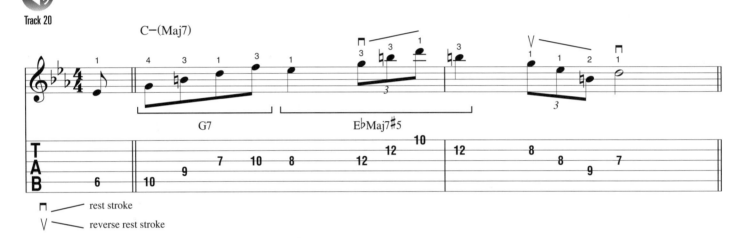

∏ ⎯⎯ rest stroke

∨ ⎯⎯ reverse rest stroke

Fig. 3.10. Melodic Phrase Using Arpeggio Substitutions for C–(Maj7)

In measure 3 of the line cliché introduced in figure 3.6, C–7 is I–7 of the C natural minor scale. Available arpeggios are the same as in the first measure of the minor line cliché: E♭Maj7 and G–7.

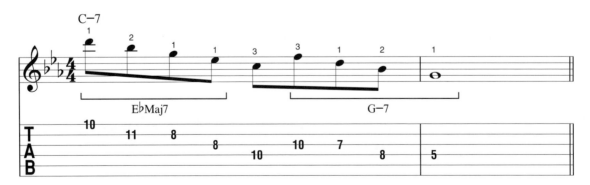

Fig. 3.11. Melodic Phrase Using Arpeggio Substitutions for C–7

In measure 4 of the line cliché, C–6 is I–6 in the C melodic minor scale. Possible substitutes are A–7♭5 and E♭Maj7♯5. Because C–6 contains the same notes as an F9 chord, another choice is to play an F7 arpeggio over C–6.

Figure 3.12 is a bebop style phrase that uses all three substitutions for C–6: F7, E♭Maj7♯5, and A–7♭5.

Track 21

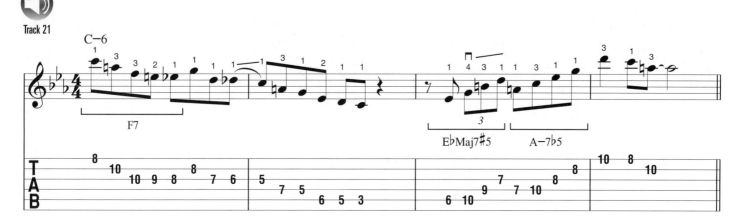

Fig. 3.12. Bebop Phrase over C–6 with Chord Substitutions F7, E♭Maj7♯5, A–7♭5

Figure 3.13 is an example of a solo over the first eight bars of "My Funny Valentine." Applying your knowledge of parallel modes in C minor, you can now improvise using arpeggio extensions and diatonic substitution to reveal the different colors of the chords in this progression.

Track 22

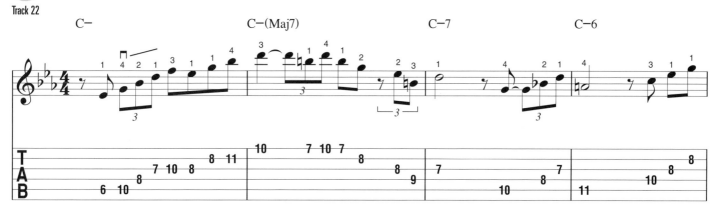

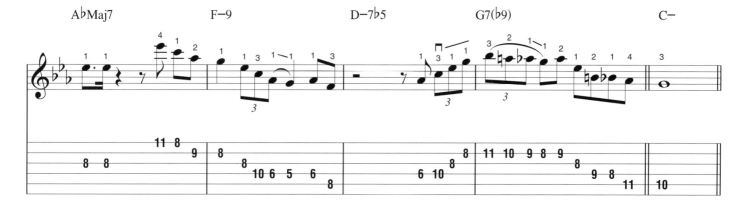

Fig. 3.13. Solo over the "My Funny Valentine" Progression

Other standard tunes that use the descending minor line cliché are Duke Ellington's "In a Sentimental Mood" and Thelonious Monk's "In Walked Bud." Mal Waldron's composition "Soul Eyes" (made famous by John Coltrane's version) is a reharmonization of the same 4-bar chord progression at the beginning of "My Funny Valentine."

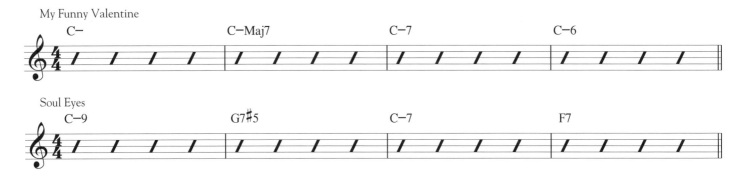

Fig. 3.14. First Four Measures of "My Funny Valentine" and "Soul Eyes"

The scales and chord substitutions are similar in both tunes yet the subtle differences in color on each chord are worthy of closer examination.

Track 23

In the second measure of "Soul Eyes," you can play an E♭Maj7♯5 arpeggio over G7 and it becomes G7(♭13); the chord has a natural 5 and tension ♭13. Note that G7(♭13) is the diatonic V7 chord in both C melodic and C harmonic minor, but the harmonic minor scale sounds more appropriate in this context, because it adds tension ♭9 (A♭) to the G7(♭13) chord.

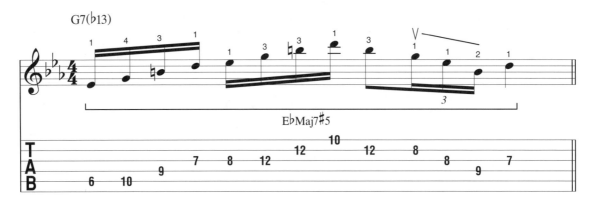

Fig. 3.15. Measure 2 of "Soul Eyes"

Most players approach measures 3 and 4 of "Soul Eyes" (C–7 / F7) simply as a II–7 / V7 in the key of B♭ major and improvise accordingly.

Otherwise if you prefer, you can play an E♭Maj7♯5 arpeggio over the F7 chord, and you will have the 13, ♭7, 9, and ♯11 of F7. Again, this is most commonly associated with the melodic minor scale because F7 is the diatonic IV7 chord in C melodic minor. The tensions on F7 are 9, ♯11, and 13.

Track 24

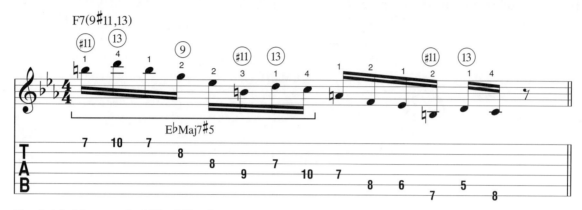

Fig. 3.16. Measure 4 of "Soul Eyes"

Track 25

FLORENCIA'S VALENTINE

Fig. 3.17. "Florencia's Valentine" (Trio Track)

CHAPTER 4

Secondary Dominants

The *primary dominant* of a major key is the V7 chord. Its root motion resolves down a perfect fifth (or up a perfect fourth) to the IMaj7 chord.

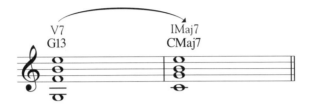

Fig. 4.1. Primary Dominant V7 Resolves to IMaj7

A *secondary dominant* is a dominant 7th chord built on a diatonic scale degree that resolves down a perfect fifth to another diatonic chord other than IMaj7.

Secondary dominants function as V7s of diatonic chords, and they are analyzed according to their expected resolutions. For example, in the key of C major, A7 resolves down a fifth to D–7, the 2nd degree of the C major scale. Therefore, A7 is V7 of II (written V7/II).

There is one primary dominant (V7/I), and there are five secondary dominants in every major key: V7/II, V7/III, V7/IV, V7/V, and V7/VI.

In the key of C major, the secondary dominants are A7 (V7/II), B7 (V7/III), C7 (V7/IV), D7 (V7/V), and E7 (V7/VI). The tensions on these dominant chords are all diatonic to the key of C major. This determines whether the dominant chord has tension 9 or ♭9, 13 or ♭13.

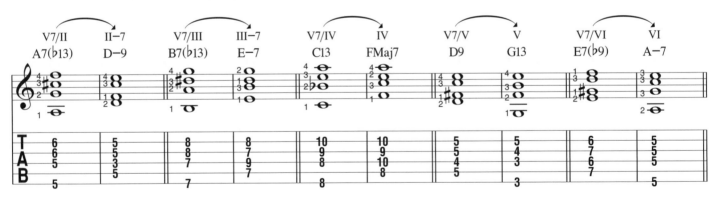

Fig. 4.2. Secondary Dominants in the Key of C Major

What about V7/VII and IV7?

There is no V7/VII because a perfect fifth above VII is a non-diatonic scale tone, ♯IV (e.g., F♯7 resolving down a fifth to B–7♭5 in the key of C). There is no secondary dominant chord built on the fourth scale degree because it resolves down a perfect fifth to the ♭VII, a non-diatonic chord (e.g., F7 resolving down a fifth to B♭ in the key of C).

Secondary Dominant Chord Scales

The scales for secondary dominants are derived from the dominant 7 chord tones with added passing notes from the relative major scale. Secondary dominant chord scales can be labeled two ways: as a modal scale from the root of the dominant chord, or as a major, melodic-minor, or harmonic-minor scale from the intended tonic of the secondary dominant. Where C7 is V7/IV and resolves to FMaj7, you can play a C Mixolydian scale (or an F major scale starting on the 5th degree) over the C7 chord.

Below is a list of the secondary dominants and their related scales in the key of C major. Memorize the function of each chord and its expected resolution. Note the available tensions on each chord.

Fig. 4.3. Secondary Dominants and Related Scales in C Major

Tip: Harmonic Minor vs. Mixolydian ♭9,♭13

Rather than using the modal name Mixolydian ♭9, ♭13, most improvisers find it easier to play a harmonic minor scale from the *intended tonic* (the chord of ultimate resolution) for V7/III and V7/VI. The intended tonic of a chord is where you expect the chord to resolve. The same concept applies to V7/II. It's easier to think of playing a melodic minor scale from the intended tonic, rather than the Mixolydian ♭13 scale. Either way, it's important to memorize the available tensions for each secondary dominant chord, both for improvising and for chordal accompaniment.

In figure 4.3, five secondary dominants were analyzed in the key of C major. Another way to learn the scales and related tensions for secondary dominants is to take one chord and analyze its function as a secondary dominant in five different keys.

As shown in Figure 4.4, C7 could be V7/IV in the key of C, V7/V in the key of B♭, V7/VI in the key of A♭, V7/II in the key of E♭, and V7/III in the key of D♭ major.

The intended tonic of C7 is always F, but the scale will change according to the function of C7 in each key. The three scale choices for C7 will be F major (C Mixolydian), F melodic minor (C Mixolydian ♭13), or F harmonic minor (C Mixolydian ♭9, ♭13).

Figure 4.4 is a chart with C7 as a secondary dominant in five keys. Note how the available tensions on C7 change according to its function in each key.

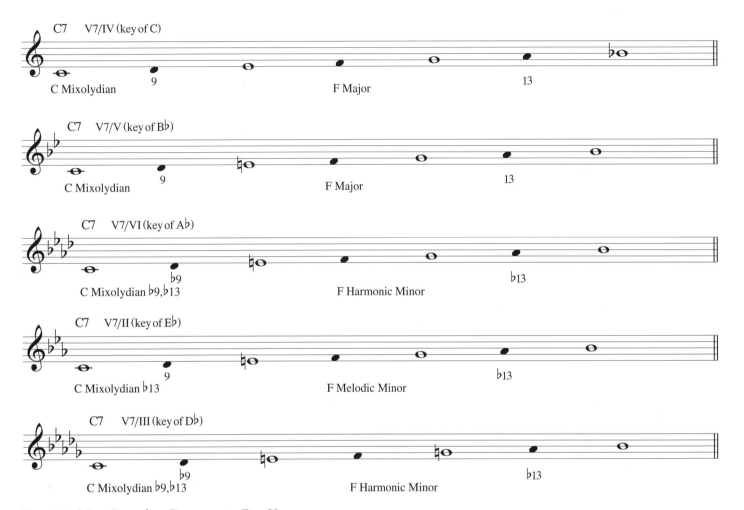

Fig. 4.4. C7 as Secondary Dominant in Five Keys

Quick Reference Chart for Secondary Dominants and Related Scales

Once you have memorized this chart, you can easily transpose it to other keys.

Scale degree	Function	Scale from Intended Tonic/Modal Scale Name
I7	V7/IV	Major/Mixolydian
II7	V7/V	Major/Mixolydian
III7	V7/VI	Harmonic Minor/Mixolydian ♭9, ♭13
VI7	V7/II	Melodic Minor/Mixolydian ♭13
VII7	V7/III	Harmonic Minor/Mixolydian ♭9, ♭13

Fig. 4.5. Secondary Dominant Quick Reference

Melodic Example: Improvising over Secondary Dominants

The following 16-bar example contains V7/II, V7/III, and V7/VI. The melody reflects the scales for each of these secondary dominants and is intended for practice to help you hear the chord-scale relationships.

Track 26

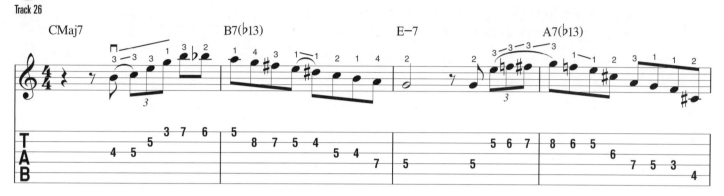

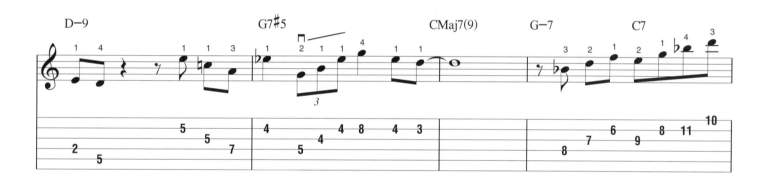

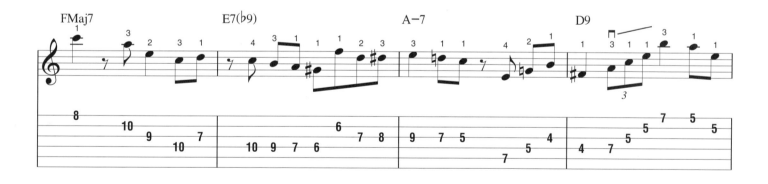

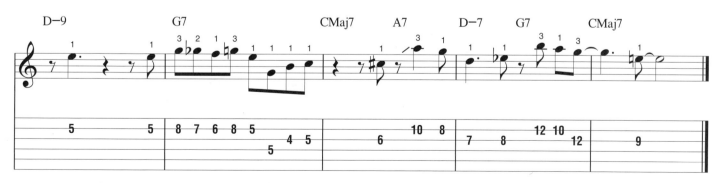

Fig. 4.6. Secondary Dominant Melodic Example

V7(♭9)/II

The scale for V7/II has a natural 9th degree, but most players use tension ♭9 on this chord because V7/II sounds harmonically similar to the #I°7 chord. Both #I°7 and V7/II resolve to II–7 (see chapter 8, page 66). When you add tension ♭9 to V7/II, the scale becomes harmonic minor from the intended tonic. In the key of C major, A7(♭9) (V7[♭9]/II) resolves to D–7 and takes a D harmonic minor scale (A Mixolydian [♭9, ♭13]).

Fig. 4.7. V7/II with Tension ♭9

Tensions ♭9, #9, ♭13 over V7/II, V7/III, and V7/VI

The two other secondary dominants that take a harmonic minor scale from the intended tonic chord are V7/III and V7/VI. Together with V7/II, all three resolve to diatonic minor 7 chords and sound like temporary V7(♭9) chords in harmonic minor. The available tensions on these secondary dominants are ♭9 and ♭13. In addition, you can also add tension #9. Here are melodic examples using ♭9, #9, and ♭13.

Track 27

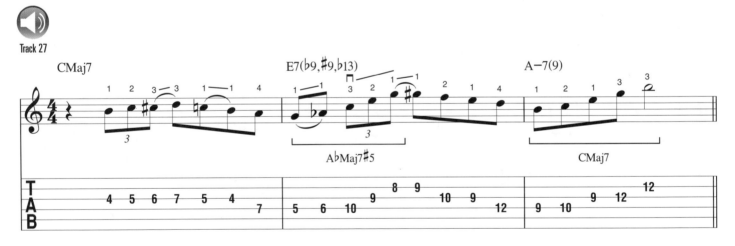

Fig. 4.8. Melodic Example with Tensions ♭9,#9,♭13 over V7/VI

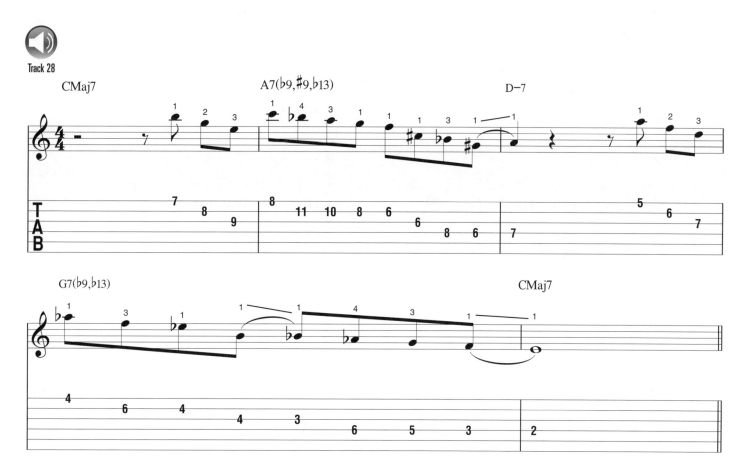

Fig. 4.9. Melodic Example with Tensions ♭9,♯9, ♭13 over V7/II

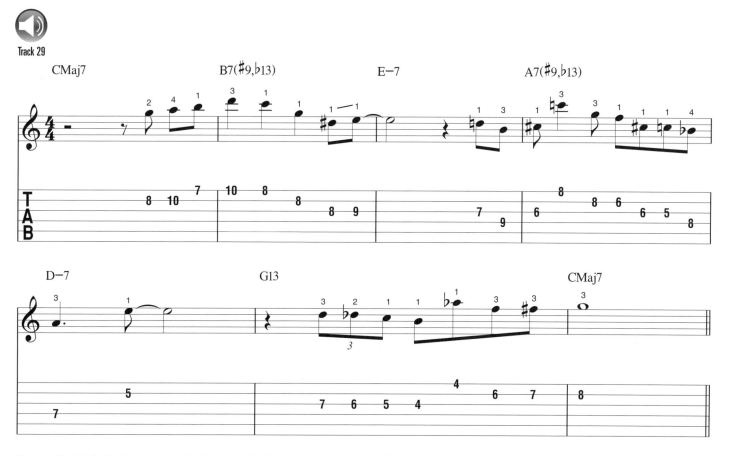

Fig. 4.10. Melodic Example with Tensions ♭9,♯9,♭13 over V7/III and V7/II

Secondary Dominants and Related II–7 Chords

Secondary dominants can be preceded by their related II–7 without changing the scale for the secondary dominant chord. The related II–7 chord for V7/VI, V7/II, and V7/III becomes a minor 7♭5 to reflect the scale for these secondary dominants.

Figures 4.11 to 4.16 are examples of secondary dominants and their related II–7 chords in the key of C major. A bracket is used to connect the II–7 and V7 chords together, and an arrow indicates the resolution to a diatonic chord.

V7/IV

Track 30

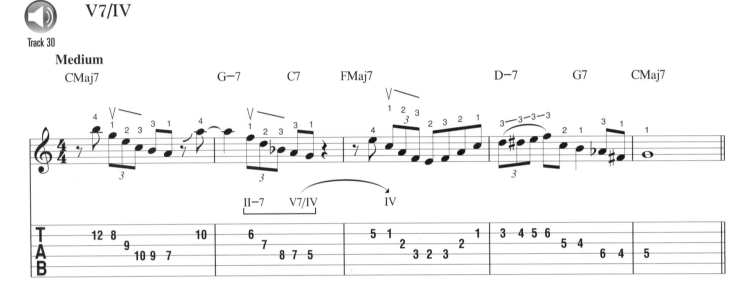

Fig. 4.11. Melodic Example of V7/IV and Related II–7 Chord

V7/V

Track 31

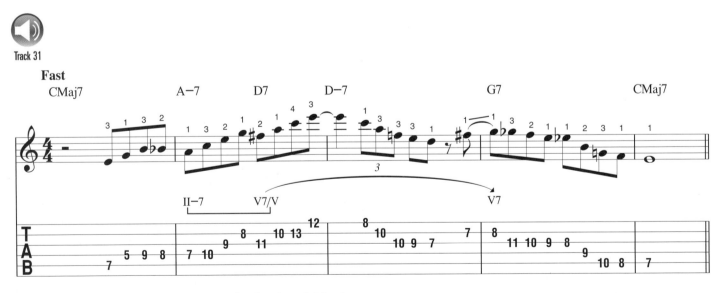

Fig. 4.12. Melodic Example of V7/V and Related II–7 Chord

V7/VI

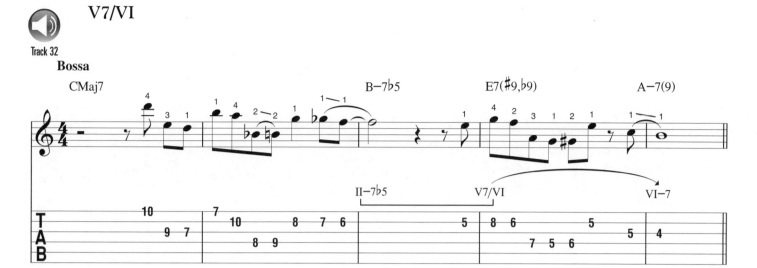

Fig. 4.13. Melodic Example of V7/VI and Related II–7 Chord

V7/II

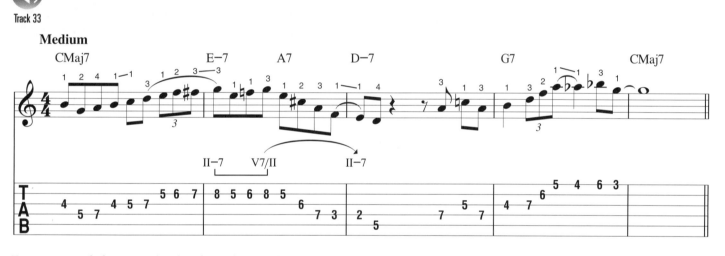

Fig. 4.14. Melodic Example of V7/II and Related II–7 Chord

When playing tension ♭9 on V7/II, the related II–7 chord is changed to II–7(♭5).

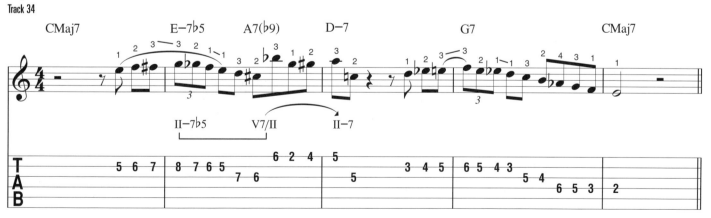

Fig. 4.15. Melodic Example of V7(♭9)/II and Related II–7♭5 Chord

V7/III

Track 35

SECONDARY SCHOOL

Fig. 4.16. "Secondary School" Melodic Example of V7/III and Related II–7 Chord (Trio Track)

TIME AND AGAIN

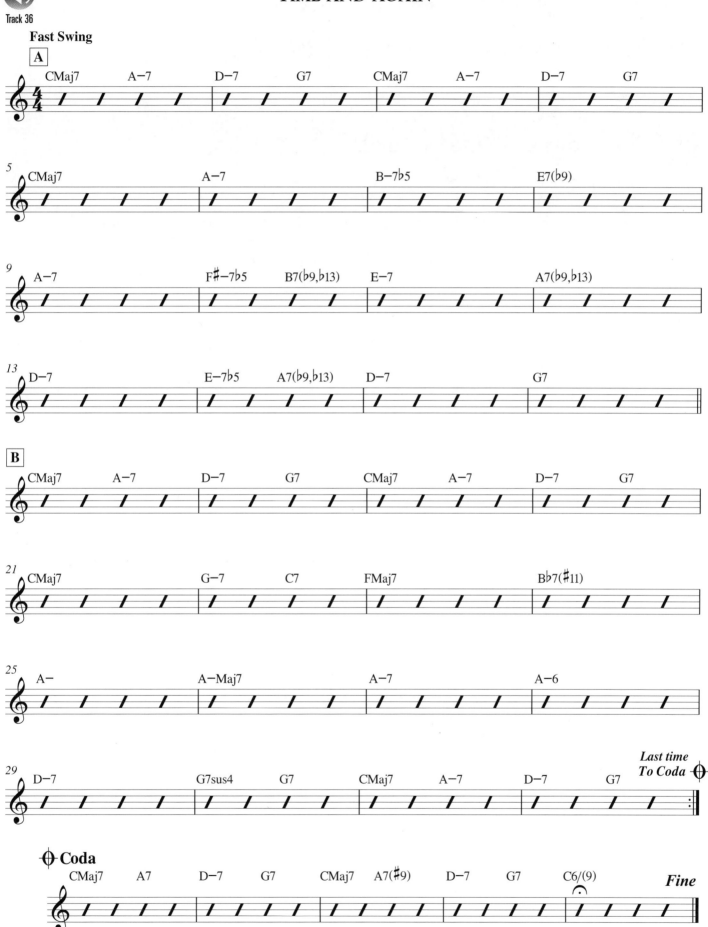

Fig. 4.17. "Time and Again" (Trio Track)

CHAPTER 5

Improvising over Minor Chords

Tensions on Minor Chords

Tension 11

All minor chords have a natural 4th scale degree (tension 11). This is true for minor triads, minor 7, minor 6, minor 7♭5, and minor (major7) chords. There is no ♯11 available on minor 7 chords because the ♯11 is enharmonically the same note as the ♭5 of a −7♭5 chord.

Fig. 5.1. Tension 11 on −6, −(Maj7), −7, and −7♭5 Chords

Tension 9

The 9th degree on diatonic minor 7 chords (II−7, III−7, and VI−7) is determined by the relative major key. II−7 and VI−7 have an available tension 9, but the 9 is not an available tension on the III−7 chord because it's a non-diatonic note in the related major key. The ♭9 is available as a passing tone on III−7 and can be used in creative melodic ways, even if it's not a stable sounding note on the chord.

Figure 5.2 illustrates how this works for III−7, VI−7, and II−7 in the key of C major.

Fig. 5.2. III−7, VI−7 and II−7 in the Key of C Major

Here is a melodic phrase using the diatonic ♭9th degree as a scale tone on III–7 and tension natural 9 on VI–7 and II–7. Note: on A–7, the B natural is tension 9 and the B♭ that follows is a chromatic passing tone. This is a typical bebop line.

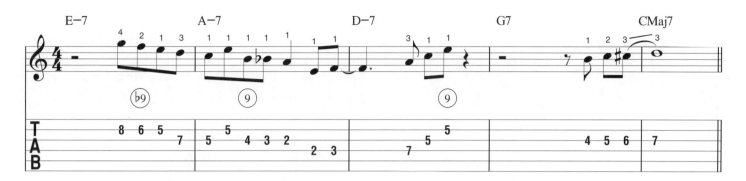

Fig. 5.3. Melodic Phrase Using Tension 9 on Diatonic Minor 7 Chords

Minor 7♭5

The 9th degree of a minor 7♭5 chord is also determined by the preceding key or tonality. The most common minor 7♭5 chord is II–7♭5 in a minor key. In the following example, D–7♭5 has a diatonic ♭9th degree (E♭), which is used as a passing tone.

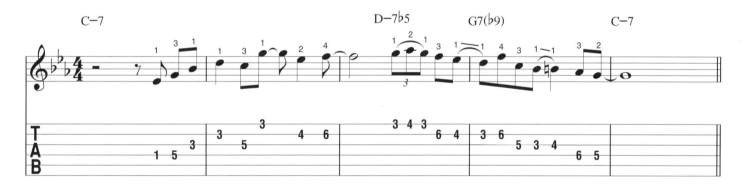

Fig. 5.4. II–7♭5 (D–7♭5) with ♭9 Used as Passing Tone

In figure 5.5, D–7♭5 is both VII–7♭5 in the key of E♭ major, and a related II–7♭5 of the secondary dominant chord, V7/VI. The corresponding scale is a diatonic E♭ major scale, or D Locrian mode, and includes the ♭9th scale degree.

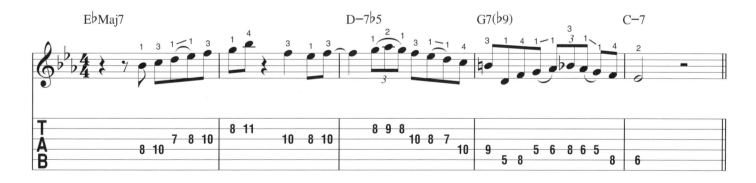

Fig. 5.5. D–7♭5 is VII–7♭5 of E♭ Major and II–7♭5 of Secondary Dominant G7(♭9)

The ♭9 is not usually considered an available tension on minor 7♭5 chords because of the half-step dissonance it creates against the chord's root. However, ♭9 is frequently played in a linear phrase when improvising. While it may create a temporary dissonance, it shouldn't be avoided or considered "unavailable." The ♭9 sounds fine when played as part of a major 7 arpeggio substitution starting on the ♭5 of the minor 7♭5 chord. For example, on A–7♭5, you can play an E♭Maj7 arpeggio (E♭, G, B♭, D). This arpeggio includes B♭, which is the ♭9 of A–7♭5.

Listen to how the ♭9 sounds when an E♭Maj7 arpeggio is played over A–7♭5 in the key of G minor.

Track 37

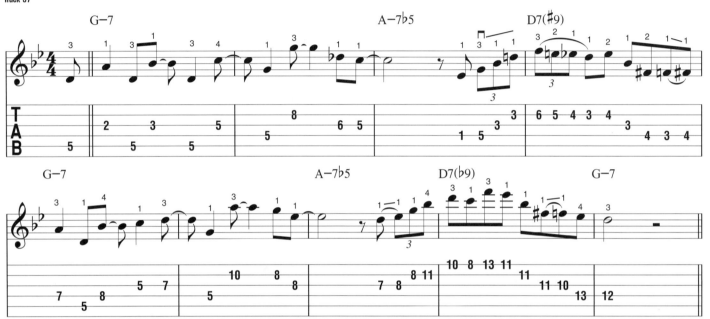

Fig. 5.6. Using ♭9 over II–7♭5 (E♭Maj7 over A–7♭5)

When a minor 7♭5 chord occurs in a major key, it opens the possibility to play a natural 9 on the chord.

On D–7♭5 in the key of C major, you can play an E natural (tension 9) because it's a diatonic scale degree from the key of C. The resulting scale is F melodic minor. The modal name for this scale is D Locrian natural 9.

In figure 5.7, D–7♭5/G7(♭9) is a II–7♭5/V7(♭9) in the key of C major.

Track 38

Fig. 5.7. Tension 9 on II–7♭5/V7(♭9) in a Major Key

Non-Diatonic Minor 7 Chords

Non-diatonic minor 7 chords are any minor 7 chord except II–7, III–7, and VI–7. They most often sound like II–7 in the key of the moment. You can play a Dorian scale with tensions 9 and 11 over all non-diatonic minor 7 chords.

Figures 5.8 and 5.9 show two melodic examples played over non-diatonic minor 7 chords in two different keys:

Track 39

Fig. 5.8. Melody with Non-Diatonic Minor 7 Chords in F Major

Track 40

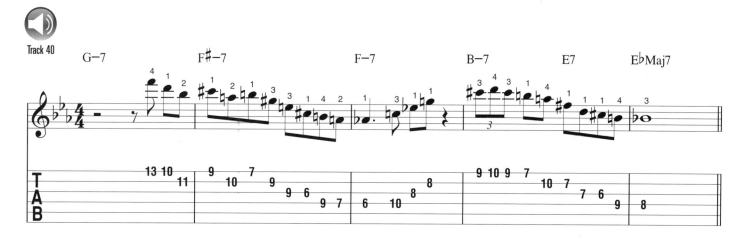

Fig. 5.9. Melody with Non-Diatonic Minor 7 Chords in E♭ Major

Minor 6 Chords

On minor 6 chords, you can play a melodic-minor scale starting from the root of the chord. In this example, C–6 is a tonic I–6 chord. The C melodic-minor scale contains both the major 6th and major 7th degrees. These tones add a bright color to the C minor chord. The progression in figure 5.10 is often found in bossa novas, especially compositions by Antonio Carlos Jobim.

Although the chord symbol is written C–6, the melodic-minor scale contains both major 6th and major 7th scale degrees, so you can also improvise using a C–(Maj7) arpeggio or its harmonic extension, E♭Maj7♯5.

Track 41

THE MERMAIDS FROM KRK

Fig. 5.10. "The Mermaids from Krk" (Trio Track)

CHAPTER 6

Common Uses of the Melodic-Minor Scale

In this chapter, you will learn the most common ways to play a melodic-minor scale over various chord types, starting from different degrees of each chord.

In classical music, the melodic-minor scale has different ascending and descending forms, but in jazz, it is the same ascending and descending. You can analyze the scale either of two ways: as a natural-minor scale with a raised 6th and 7th degree, or as a major scale with a lowered third degree.

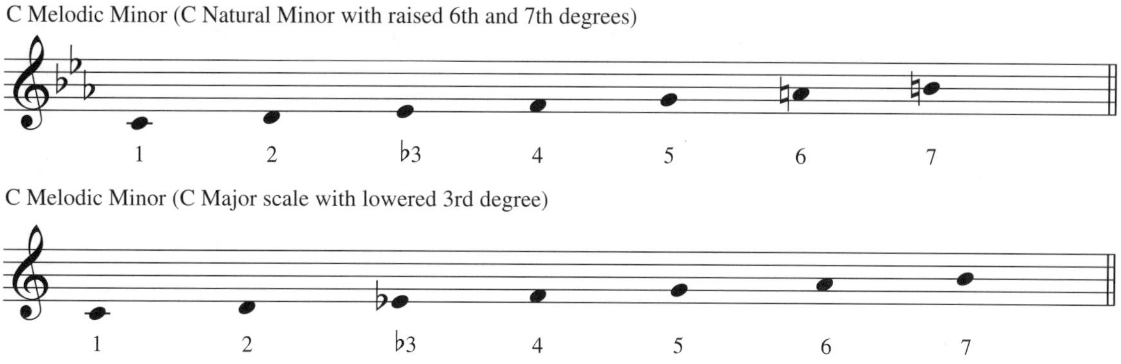

C Melodic Minor (C Natural Minor with raised 6th and 7th degrees)

C Melodic Minor (C Major scale with lowered 3rd degree)

Fig. 6.1. Two Ways to Construct the Melodic-Minor Scale

To understand how to play the melodic-minor scale and its modes over various chord types, it is important to know the diatonic chords from melodic minor (as discussed in chapter 3).

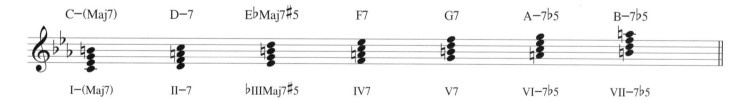

Fig. 6.2. Diatonic Chords in C Melodic Minor

Like the major scale, the melodic-minor scale generates modal names from each scale degree.

Figure 6.3 illustrates the modes of the C melodic-minor scale and the diatonic chords associated with each mode, with two important differences: the 2nd and 7th modes of the melodic-minor scale are used to improvise over chord types that are non-diatonic to the melodic-minor scale. The second mode is usually played over D7sus4(♭9) and the 7th mode is played over B7(alt). This last mode is called the altered dominant scale, Superlocrian, or diminished whole-tone scale, and will be discussed in chapter 7.

Fig. 6.3. Modes of the C Melodic-Minor Scale

Instead of thinking of the modal names while improvising, most players find it easier to play the melodic-minor scale starting from different notes in the chord (other than the root). The chord degree you start on will depend on the function of that chord in a particular key and what sound is most appropriate.

For example, A–7♭5 is VI–7♭5 of the C melodic-minor scale. Rather than thinking of the modal name A Locrian Natural 2, it's easier to play a melodic-minor scale from the ♭3rd degree of the chord. Over A–7♭5, you'll play a C melodic-minor scale, which adds tension 9 to A–7♭5 (see chapter 5, figure 5.6).

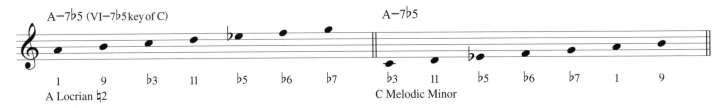

Fig. 6.4. Locrian Natural 2 Compared to a Melodic-Minor Scale from the ♭3rd Degree of a Minor 7♭5 Chord

Let's work on various applications of the melodic-minor scale by learning about subdominant minor chords.

Subdominant Minor Chords (IV Minor)

The IV chord in a major key functions harmonically as a subdominant chord. By flatting the third degree, it becomes IV minor, the subdominant minor chord.

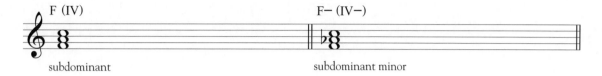

Fig. 6.5. IV and IV– / Subdominant and Subdominant Minor

The IV– chord can be either IV–7 or IV–6. When there is no ♭7th degree on the IV– chord, the major 7th degree becomes an available tension or scale tone, and the resulting scale is melodic minor from the root of the chord.

Fig. 6.6. IV–6 and F Melodic-Minor Scale

The IV–6 is similar to the I–6 chord you studied at the end of the previous chapter, except that IV–6 expands exponentially into a universe of harmonic relativity, all derived from subdominant minor and related to the melodic-minor scale.

The IV–6 is used in many standard tunes, such as "There Will Never Be Another You," "All of You," "Weaver of Dreams," and "Days of Wine and Roses," and often found in the following progression: IMaj7, V7/ IV, IVMaj7, IV–6. In the key of C major: CMaj7 / C7 / FMaj7 / F–6.

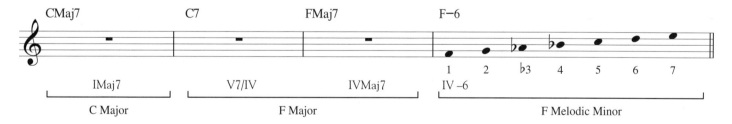

Fig. 6.7. Common Chord Progression Using IV–6

Figure 6.8 illustrates a descending chromatic guide-tone line for this progression that reflects the smoothest resolution of one chord to the next. This approach is similar to the descending chromatic line explained in chapter 3, figure 3.9.

Fig. 6.8. A Guide-Tone Line

Figure 6.9 is a melodic phrase using guide tones to connect the melody over the bar line. Two types of melodic resolution are used: indirect and double chromatic (also called "double indirect").

Track 42

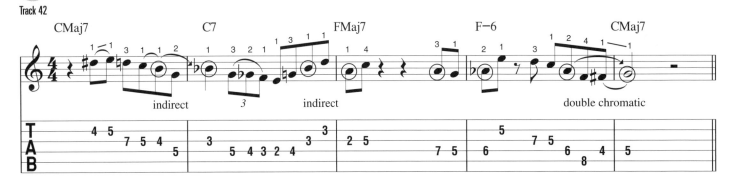

Fig. 6.9. Using Guide Tones to Connect the Melody over the Bar Line

Subdominant Minor Chords: IV–6, ♭VII7, II–7♭5

There is a relationship between melodic minor and the chords of subdominant minor. To understand how these two are interconnected, let's define the properties of subdominant minor chords.

All subdominant minor chords are harmonically related because they contain the ♭6th degree of the relative major scale. The name "subdominant minor" doesn't mean that the chord is minor. It refers to various chord types related to the IV– chord. Subdominant is a function, like tonic and dominant.

Other subdominant minor chords related to IV–6 are ♭VII7 and II–7♭5. In the key of C major, these chords are F–6 (IV–6), B♭7(9) (♭VII7[9]), and D–7♭5 (II–7♭5). Each chord contains the ♭6th degree of the C major scale (A♭) and they have exactly the same spelling except for the root of each chord.

Figure 6.10 illustrates the harmonic relationship between F–6, B♭7(9) and D–7♭5, starting with a 4-note chord voicing for all three chords, then analyzing the degrees of each chord.

Fig. 6.10. Harmonic Relationship Between F–6, B♭7(9), and D–7♭5

The common scale for all three chords is F melodic minor.

It's helpful to know the modal names for these scales, but especially important to memorize the available tensions for each chord.

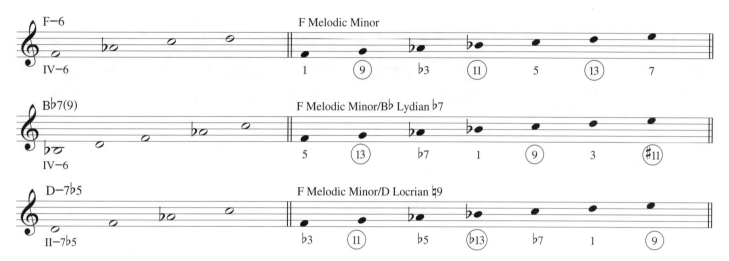

Fig. 6.11. F Melodic Minor Is Common to the Subdominant-Minor Chords of C Major

The IV–6 and ♭VII7 sound almost identical; the only difference is the bass note. These two chords are interchangeable and ♭VII7 is often used as a substitute for IV–6. The melody in measure 4 of figure 6.12 is derived from the F melodic-minor scale and can be played over B♭7 (♭VII7) or F–6 (IV–6).

Track 43

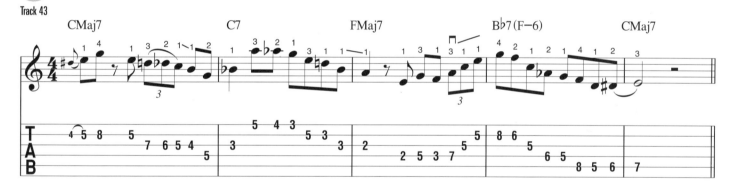

Fig. 6.12. ♭VII7 (B♭7) Can Substitute for IV–6 (F–6)

♭VII7: Tensions 9, ♯11, 13

The scale for ♭VII7 is melodic minor from the 5th degree of the chord. The available tensions are 9, ♯11, and 13. These notes form a major triad a whole step above the root of the chord.

Figure 6.13 demonstrates this approach for B♭7 in the key of C. The scale is F melodic minor. Tensions 9, ♯11, and 13 are found by playing a C major triad (C, E, G) over the B♭7 chord.

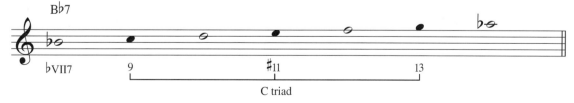

Fig. 6.13. C Major Triad Contains Tensions 9, ♯11, 13 of B♭7

Track 44

Here is an example of a melody that outlines a C major triad over Bb7 to add tensions 9, #11, and 13.

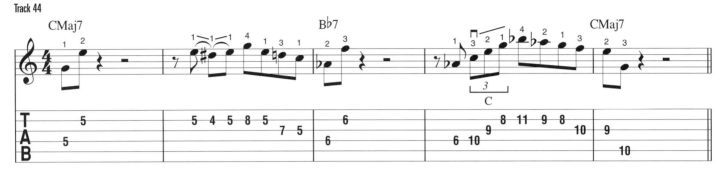

Fig. 6.14. C Major Triad Played over Bb7

Let's continue with other dominant 7th chords that use the melodic-minor scale from the 5th degree.

IV7

In the key of C major, F7 is the IV7 chord. The corresponding scale is melodic minor from the 5th degree of the chord (C melodic minor). The modal name is F Lydian b7. Available tensions are 9, #11, and 13.

Fig. 6.15. F Lydian b7 = C Melodic Minor

Although C melodic minor and F Lydian b7 contain the same notes, most guitarists find it easier to visualize the notes on the fretboard by thinking of the melodic-minor scale. With the fingerings you already know for the major scale, flatting the 3rd degree will instantly give you enough positions of the melodic-minor scale to cover the entire fretboard.

Track 45

Fig. 6.16. Melodic Minor Scale from the 5th Degree of the IV7 Chord

Unaltered Dominant 7 Chords with Non-Diatonic Roots

Playing a melodic-minor scale from the 5th degree of a dominant 7 chord can be applied to all unaltered dominant 7 chords with non-diatonic roots. The available tensions are always 9, #11, and 13.

"Unaltered" dominant 7 means that the 9th and 5th degrees are not raised or lowered. In other words, there is no ♭9, #9, ♭5(*), or #5 present in the chord.

The non-diatonic dominant 7 chords commonly found in a major key (don't forget enharmonic spellings) are: ♭II7, ♭III7, ♭V7, ♭VI7, and ♭VII7. In the key of C major, the non-diatonic chords D♭7, E♭7, G♭7, A♭7, and B♭7 all contain tensions 9, #11, and 13.

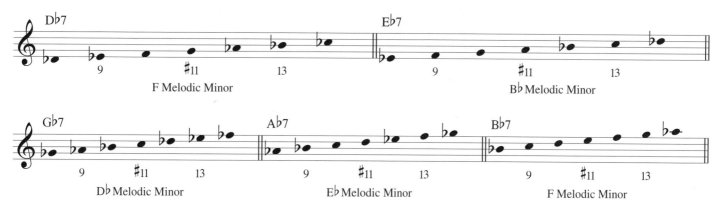

Fig. 6.17. Non-Diatonic Dominant 7 Chords in C Major Have Tensions 9, #11, and 13

Here is a melodic example that demonstrates this point with non-diatonic dominant 7 chords in the key of C major. E♭7, D♭7, B♭7, and A♭7 all have tensions 9, #11, and 13.

Track 46

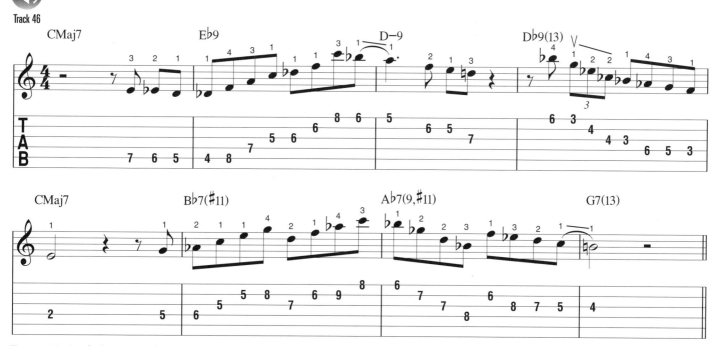

Fig. 6.18. Melodic Example Using Non-Diatonic Dominant 7 Chords

(*) The ♭5 of a dominant 7 chord is enharmonically the same note as #11; however, #11 implies that there is a natural 5th degree in the chord.

Dominant 7 chords with non-diatonic roots also appear in minor keys. The most frequent are ♭VI7 and ♭II7. The following progression shows both in the key of D minor:

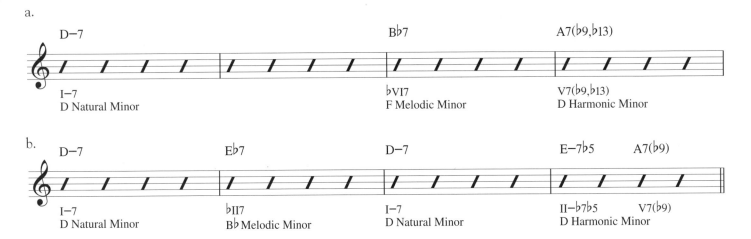

Fig. 6.19. Melodic Minor Scale from the 5th Degree of ♭VI7 and ♭II7 in D Minor

V7(♭13) Melodic Minor Scale from the 4th Degree

On V7(♭13) in a major key, you can play a melodic-minor scale from the 4th degree of the chord. For C7(♭13) in the key of F major, play an F melodic-minor scale. The modal name for this scale is C Mixolydian ♭6 (also called C Mixolydian ♭13) and includes tension natural 9 and ♭13 of the C7 chord.

The ♭13th is enharmonically the same note as ♯5. The difference is, ♭13 implies that the chord has a natural 5th degree.

Fig. 6.20. Using Melodic Minor from 4th Degree on V7(♭13) in F Major

The Mixolydian ♭13 scale is most often used on the V7 chord in a II–7 / V7 / I progression in a major key. The ♭13th adds a bluesy sound to melodic lines because it's the same as the ♭3rd of the relative major scale.

Figure 6.21, in the key of F major, uses an F melodic-minor scale over C7(♭13) in measure 2. And in measure 6, the melody outlines F melodic minor with chromatic passing tones.

Track 47

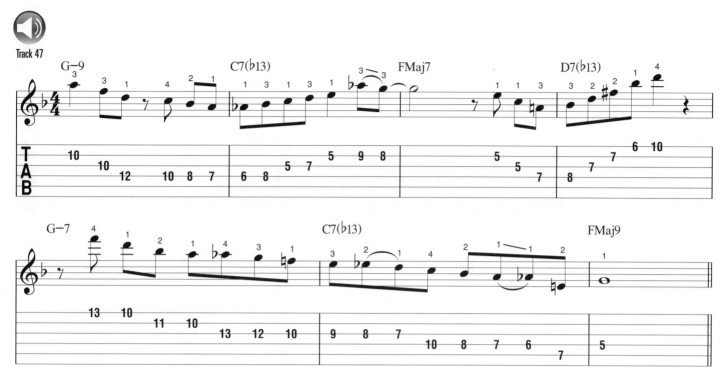

Fig. 6.21. Using Melodic Minor/Mixolydian ♭13 over V7(♭13)

On V7(♭13) in a major key, you can use diatonic substitution to play arpeggios from the melodic-minor scale. For G7(♭13) in the key of C, you can play an E♭Maj7♯5 arpeggio which includes both the natural 5th and ♭13th degrees of the G7 chord.

Track 48

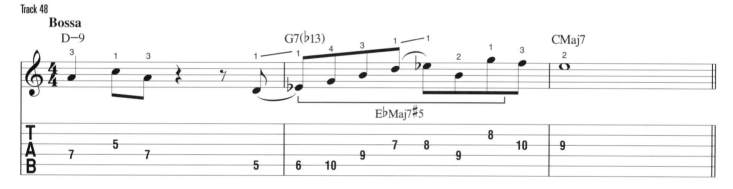

Fig. 6.22. Diatonic Substitution: ♭IIIMaj7♯5 Arpeggio for V7(♭13)

V7 (♭9, 13) Melodic Minor Scale from the ♭7th Degree

In chapter 4, you learned how to play a melodic-minor scale from the ♭3rd degree of the II–7♭5 chord in a major key. So, for D–7♭5 (in the key of C major), you could play an F melodic-minor scale. The F melodic-minor scale can also be played over the G7(♭9) (melodic minor from the ♭7th degree of the chord). Harmonically, the V7 chord then sounds like G13 (♭9, ♯9).

The F melodic-minor scale doesn't contain the major 3rd degree of G7 (B), but the ♯9 adds a bluesy sound to the chord.

Here is an example of an F melodic minor scale played over G13(♭9). An A♭Maj7#5 arpeggio substitution is derived from the F melodic-minor scale and makes the G7 chord sound like G13sus4(♭9, #9).

Track 49

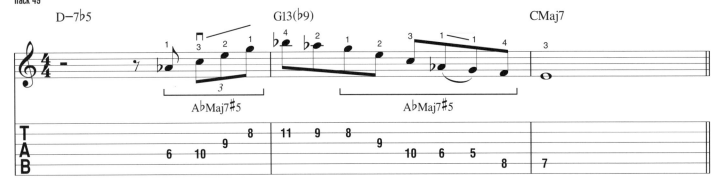

Fig. 6.23. F Melodic Minor over G7(♭9,13)

Theory of Harmonic Relativity

To understand more about playing melodic-minor scales starting on different chord degrees, let's look at the harmonic relationship between chords.

The example below contains a harmonic equation of different chords with the same notes, except for the bass. I call this the Theory of Harmonic Relativity. The scale for one chord in the equation applies to other chords in the same equation.

The first example is in the key of C major. The equation starts with a C6 chord. The same four notes also spell A–7, FMaj7(9), and D9(sus4). The common scale for all chords in this equation is C major.

C6 = A–7 = FMaj9 = D9sus4

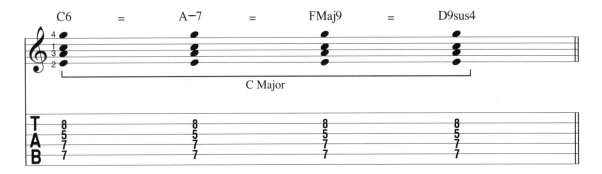

Fig. 6.24. Chords in C Major with the Same Notes

The next example demonstrates the theory of harmonic relativity using the melodic-minor scale. By flatting the third degree of C6 (from the previous equation), the chord becomes C–6 and all the other chords in the equation are changed accordingly. The common scale for all these chords is C melodic minor.

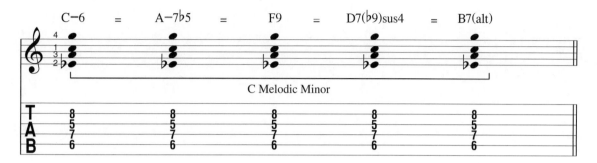

Fig. 6.25. Chords with Similar Spelling Using the C Melodic Minor Scale

This harmonic equation demonstrates the various ways of playing a melodic-minor scale starting on different degrees of each chord.

C–6:	melodic minor from the root
A–7♭5:	melodic minor from the ♭3rd
F9 (♯11, 13):	melodic minor from the 5th
D7sus4 (♭9, 13):	melodic minor from the ♭7th
B7 (altered):	melodic minor from the ♭9th

Melodic Minor Quick Reference

This quick reference chart shows common uses of the melodic-minor scale starting on different chord degrees.

Chord	Melodic-Minor Scale
I–6/IV–6	melodic-minor scale from the root of the chord
II–7♭5	melodic-minor scale from the ♭3rd of the chord
♭VII7	melodic-minor scale from the 5th degree of the chord
IV7	melodic-minor scale from the 5th degree of the chord
V7(alt)	melodic-minor scale from the ♭9th of the chord
V7(♭13)	melodic-minor scale from the 4th of the chord or from the intended tonic
V7sus4 (♭9, 13)	melodic-minor scale from the ♭7th of the chord

I DREAM OF NICA (first 16 bars)

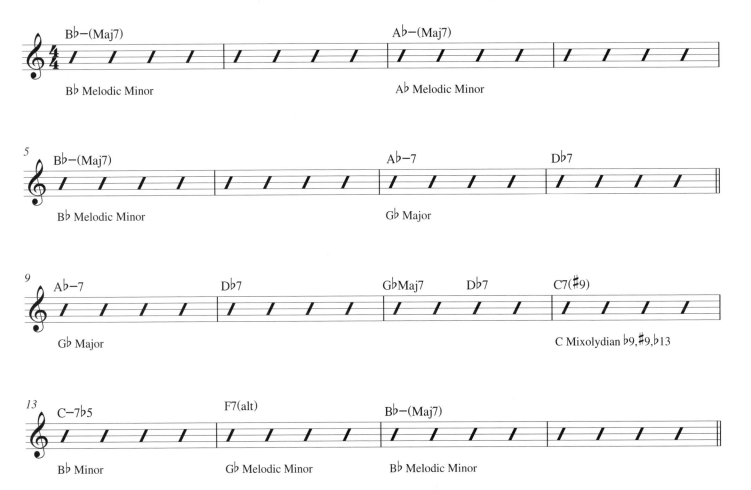

Fig. 6.26. *"I Dream of Nica" (First 16 Bars)*

A BRIDGE IN CHELSEA (first 8 bars)

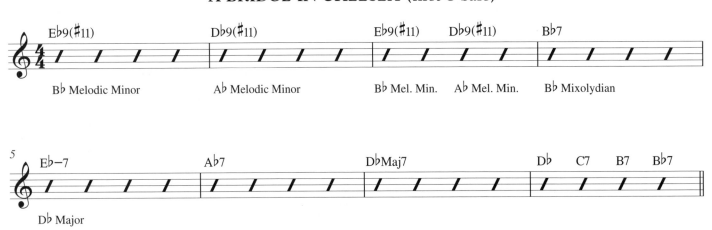

Fig. 6.27. *"A Bridge in Chelsea" (First 8 Bars)*

TENDER LEE

Fig. 6.28. "Tender Lee" (Trio Track)

CHAPTER 7

♭II7 and V7(alt) Chords

II–7 / ♭II7 / IMaj7

The II–7 / ♭II7 / IMaj7 progression is a common cadence in which the ♭II7 chord functions as a substitution for the V7. The chords ♭II7 and V7 are related because they share the same tritone, and both work as dominant chords resolving to the IMaj7 chord.

Figure 7.1 illustrates how the 3rd and 7th of each chord are used to create guide tone lines that outline the sound of both ♭II7 and V7.

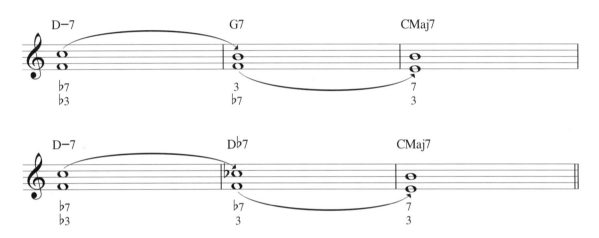

Fig. 7.1. Guide Tones in II–7 / ♭II7 / IMaj7 in C Major

In chapter 6, you learned that ♭II7 is a dominant 7 chord with a non-diatonic root. The corresponding scale is melodic minor from the 5th degree of the chord. The scale for D♭7 (♭II7) is A♭ melodic minor, or D♭ Lydian ♭7, and the tensions are 9, ♯11, and 13.

Fig. 7.2. Melodic Minor Scale from the 5th Degree of ♭II7

Melodic Lines for II–7 / ♭II7 / IMaj7

The following examples show how to create phrases with the A♭ melodic minor scale over D♭7 using guide tone lines to connect the changes. The guide tones are circled, and melodic resolution is indicated by arrows. The last example introduces another guide tone line: the 5th of D♭7 (A♭) resolves to the 5th of CMaj7 (G) by a double-chromatic approach from below.

Track 51

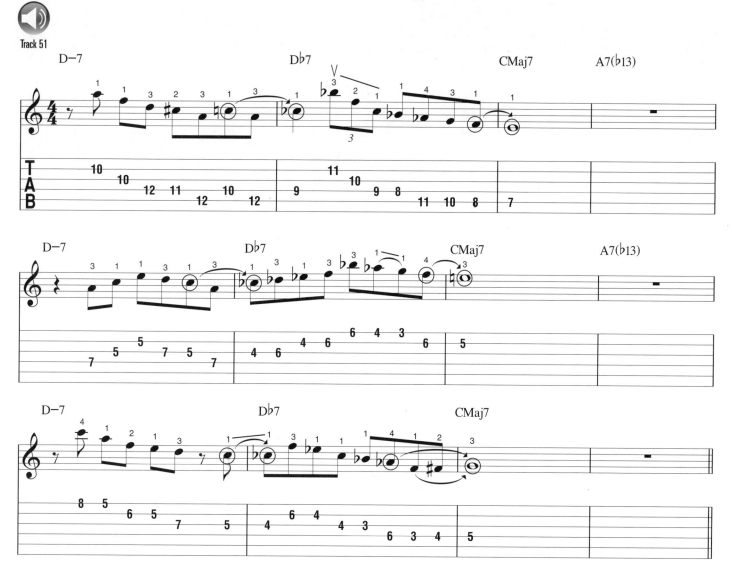

Fig. 7.3. Phrases for II–7 / ♭II7 / IMaj7 in C Major

Figure 7.4 offers more melodic phrases to play over the II–7 / ♭II7 / I progression in four different keys. This will help you acquire a greater awareness of the sound of this progression and more specifically, the sound of the melodic-minor scale over the ♭II7 chord. Play these lines with the harmonic accompaniment, and note the different guide-tone resolutions from the ♭II7 to the I chord.

Track 52

Fig. 7.4. Phrases for II–7 / ♭II7 / IMaj7 in Four Keys

V7 Altered Chords

When a dominant chord is altered (alt), both the 5th and 9th degrees have been raised or lowered by one half step. Altered dominant chords appear most frequently in II–7 / V7(alt) / IMaj7 progressions, where chromatic alterations to the 5th and 9th degrees of the V7 chord create darker sounding dominants with more complex possibilities of resolution to the I chord, both harmonically and melodically.

V7(alt) chords are constructed from the following notes: Root, 3rd, ♭5 or ♯5, ♭7, ♭9, or ♯9.

Fig. 7.5. G7(alt) Chord Construction

When choosing voicings, or improvising over V7(alt) chords, it can be hard to keep track of all the possible tensions, but there is a very easy way to solve this problem: playing the ♭II7 over the V7 chord automatically gives you all the altered tensions for the V7.

When playing D♭7 (♭II7) as a substitute for G7 (V7alt), the natural tensions on D♭7 are always the altered tensions on G7.

There are four possible G7(alt) chords: G7♭5(♭9), G7♯5(♭9), G7♭5(♯9), and G7♯5(♯9). Figure 7.6 shows their relationship to D♭7.

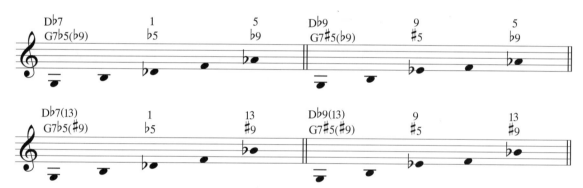

Fig. 7.6. Possible Combinations of G7(alt) and D♭7

Guitar voicings for altered chords usually have only four notes (minus the root). The tritone is usually on the bottom of the voicing, with two altered tensions on top.

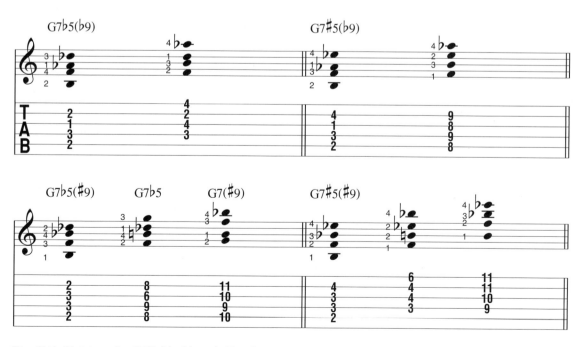

Fig. 7.7. Voicings for G7(alt) Altered Chords

Improvising over V7 Altered Chords

On V7(alt) chords, you can play a melodic-minor scale from the ♭9th degree of the chord (a half step above the root of the chord). This produces the altered-dominant scale with tensions ♭9, ♯9, ♭5, and ♯5.

For G7(alt), play an A♭ melodic-minor scale starting on G. The modal name for this scale is G altered dominant, also called the "Superlocrian" mode, or diminished whole-tone scale. The third degree of G7 (B) is enharmonically written as C♭ in the A♭ melodic-minor scale.

Fig. 7.8. A♭ Melodic Minor over a G7(alt) Chord

Figure 7.9 shows the scales for V7(alt) chords in different keys, with a comparison between the "altered-dominant" scale starting on the root of the V7 and the melodic-minor scale one half step above the root of the chord. The major 3rd degree of each scale is written with enharmonic spelling. For example, E natural is the 3rd degree of C7, instead of F♭, the minor third degree of the D♭ melodic-minor scale.

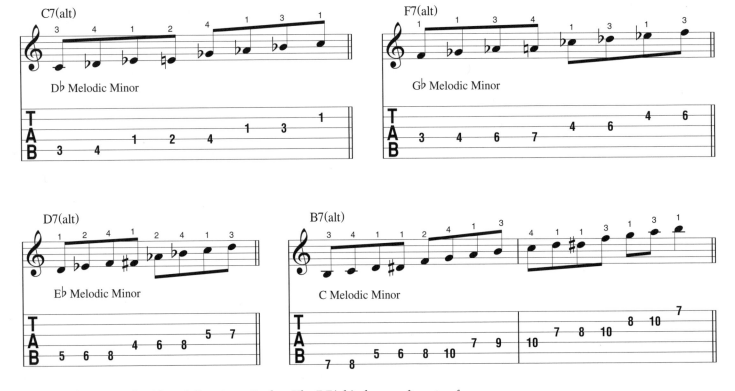

Fig. 7.9. Fingerings for Altered-Dominant Scales. The B7(alt) shows a fingering for two octaves.

Melodic Lines for II–7 / V7(alt) / IMaj7

D♭7 (♭II7) and G7(alt) (V7alt) are interchangeable, and the common scale for both is A♭ melodic minor. When improvising over G7(alt), it's easier to create melodic lines if you simply think of playing the same lines you learned for D♭7.

To help you make the connection between V7(alt) and ♭II7, go back to the last section on "II–7 / ♭II7 / I," and play those melodic examples over II–7 / V7(alt) / I.

Track 53

Here are several new examples that you can practice to get your ears accustomed to this sound.

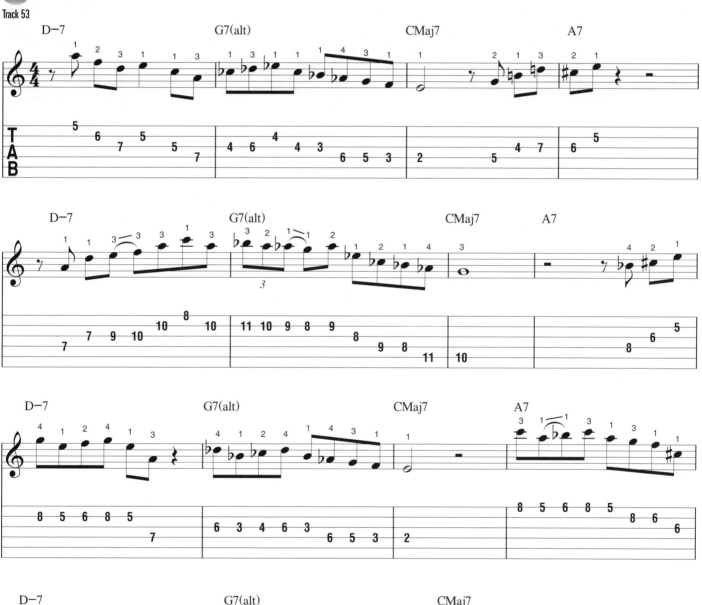

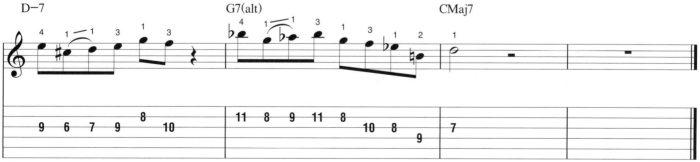

Fig. 7.10. D♭7 Lines over G7(alt)

Tritone-Substitute Chords

Other chords besides the V7 can be altered by playing a tritone substitute. A *tritone-substitute* chord is a dominant chord a tritone away from the original chord. In this example, V7/II (D7) becomes V7(alt)/II by playing the tritone substitute, A♭7.

Track 54

In figure 7.11, the tritone substitute chords are in parenthesis. The scale for any altered dominant is melodic minor, a half step above the root of the original chord.

Fig. 7.11. *Melodic Example of Tritone Substitute Chords*

Track 55

Here is another example, in the key of E♭ major. This progression is a turnaround using tritone substitute chords: II–7 / V7(alt) / III–7 / V7(alt) / II–7.

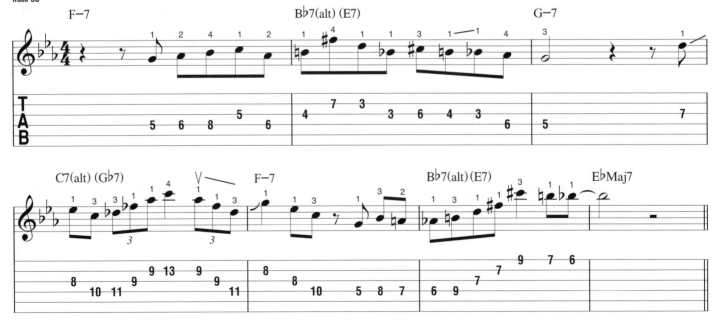

Fig. 7.12. *Tritone Substitute Dominant on Turnaround Progression*

Figure 7.13 (with the trio track) is a turnaround progression that you can use to practice playing tritone substitutions over dominant 7 altered chords.

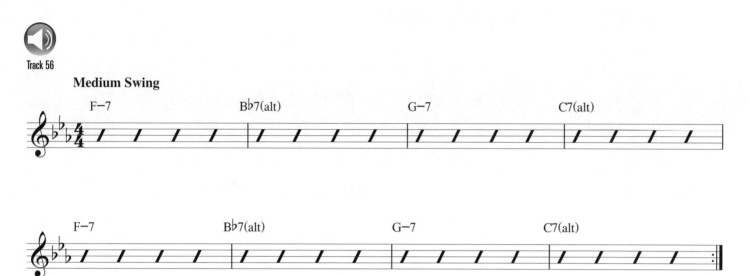

Fig. 7.13. *Substitute Dominants Practice Progression (Trio Track)*

CHAPTER 8

Diminished 7th Chords

The diminished 7th chord is a 4-note chord built in minor third intervals comprising chord degrees 1, ♭3, ♭5, and ♭♭7.

Fig. 8.1. C Diminished 7th Chord

With enharmonic spelling, diminished 7th chords can be simplified to avoid the use of double flats. The ♭♭7th degree is enharmonically the same as the 6th. By converting the B♭♭ to an A natural, the C°7 chord can be written as follows:

Fig. 8.2. Enharmonic Spelling of C°7 Chord

Because of its symmetrical construction, any one of the four notes in a diminished 7th chord can function as the root. Therefore, C°7 is also E♭°7, G♭°7, and A°7.

Fig. 8.3. Diminished Chords Originating from C°7

Because each diminished 7th chord has four possible tonics, all twelve keys are contained within three diminished 7th chords: C°7, C♯°7, and D°7.

C°7 = E♭°7 = G♭°7 = A°7

C♯°7 = E°7 = G°7 = B♭°7

D°7 = F°7 = A♭°7 = B°7

Figure 8.4 illustrates four different guitar voicings for diminished 7th chords. Remember, any note in the chord can be the root, so you can play four inversions of each of these voicings.

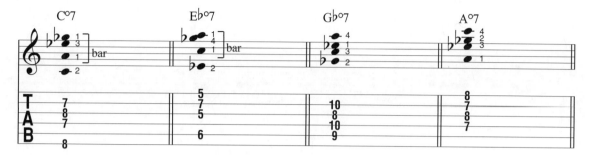

Fig. 8.4. Common Voicings for Diminished 7th Chords

Improvising with Diminished 7th Arpeggios

The easiest way to improvise over diminished 7th chords is to play a diminished 7th arpeggio. Figure 8.5 shows two phrases using common fingerings for diminished 7th arpeggios. Remember that since any note can be the root of the chord, it doesn't matter which note you start on. These phrases could be played over C♯°7, E°7, G°7, or B♭°7.

Fig. 8.5. Phrases Using Common Fingerings for Diminished 7th Arpeggios

♯I°7

One of the most common diminished 7th chords is ♯I°7. It is found in the progression IMaj7 / ♯I°7 / II–7, in the beginning of Gershwin's "Strike Up the Band" and in the bridges of "The Way You Look Tonight" and "Polkadots and Moonbeams."

In the key of C major, C♯°7 is ♯I°7 and resolves upward by a half step to D–7 (II–7). Chromatic guide-tone lines create strong resolution between the chords in this progression.

Fig. 8.6. Chromatic Guide-Tone Lines

You can build melodic phrases using the two fingerings for diminished 7th arpeggios in figure 8.5 connected by the guide tones illustrated in the previous example.

Track 57

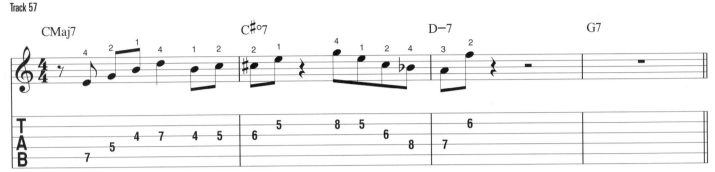

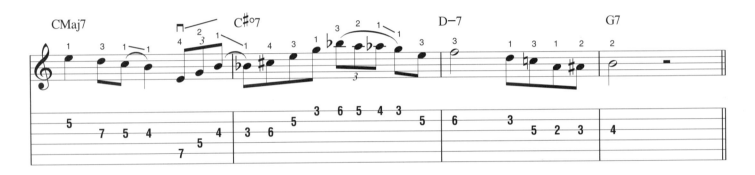

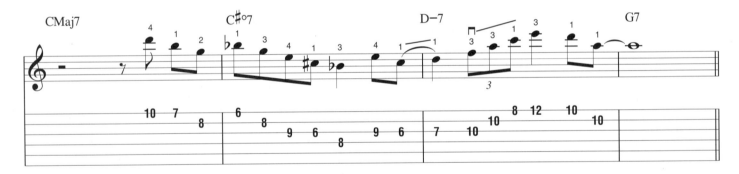

Fig. 8.7. Melodic Examples for ♯I°7

♭III°7

Another common function of the diminished 7th chord is ♭III°7. In figure 8.8, E♭°7 is ♭III°7 in the key of C major and resolves down one half step to D–7 (II–7). A descending chromatic guide-tone line can be used to connect the chords.

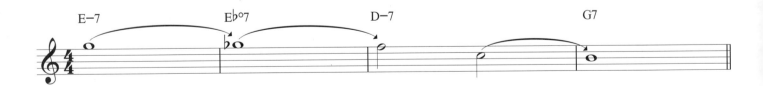

Fig. 8.8. Descending Chromatic Guide-Tone Line

The melody in figure 8.9 uses the chromatic guide-tone line from figure 8.8. Note the octave displacement of this line in the third measure where G♭ resolves down a half step to F.

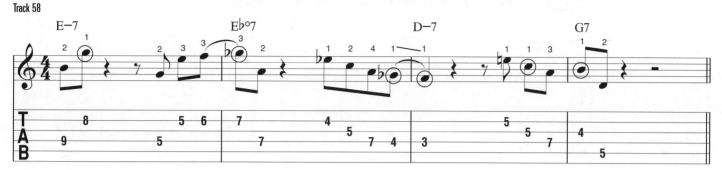

Fig. 8.9. Melody Using Chromatic Guide Tones

Diminished 7th Chords as Secondary Dominants

A diminished 7th chord contains two tritones, which allow for diminished 7th chords to have dominant function.

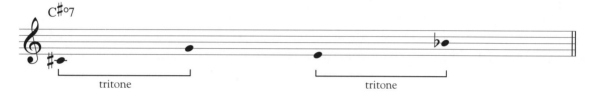

Fig. 8.10. Diminished 7th Chords Contain Two Tritones

A diminished 7th chord can be the upper structure of a dominant 7(♭9) chord. For example, C♯°7 is the upper structure of A7(♭9).

Fig. 8.11. C♯°7 as the Upper Structure of A7(♭9)

♯I°7 = V7(♭9)/II

♯I°7 and V7(♭9)/II both resolve to the II–7 chord and sound the same, except for the root motion. Play the following progression, first with C♯°7 and then with A7(♭9), and you will hear the similar sound of these two chords.

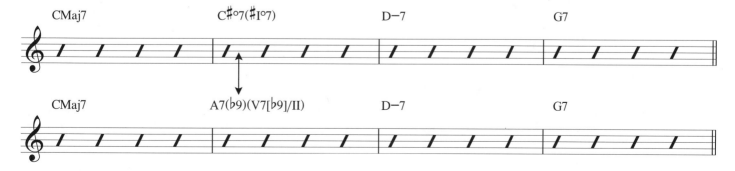

Fig. 8.12. C♯°7 and A7(♭9) Sound the Same Except for the Root Motion

Improvising with Harmonic Minor Scales

Because of the interchangeable function of ♯I°7 and V7(♭9)/II, the scale for both chords is the same. You can play D harmonic minor over both A7(♭9) and C♯°7. This is perfectly logical when you consider that C♯°7 is also the diatonic VII°7 chord in the key of D harmonic minor.

Fig. 8.13. Harmonic Minor Starting from 5th and 7th Degrees

V7(♭9,♯9)

All dominant 7th chords with tension ♭9 can simultaneously have tension ♯9. Most improvisers instinctively play tensions ♭9 and ♯9 together on dominant chords, and this approach can also be used for diminished 7th chords. By adding tension ♯9 to the V7 chord, the harmonic minor scale becomes an 8-tone scale, and is also called Mixolydian ♭9, ♯9, ♭13. (See page 34 for a review of secondary dominant chord scales.)

When played over a diminished 7th chord, this 8-tone scale adds tension major 7, an available tension on all diminished 7th chords.

Figure 8.14 compares A7(♭9,♯9) and C♯°7 (with tension major 7), followed by two melodic examples that work equally well for both chords.

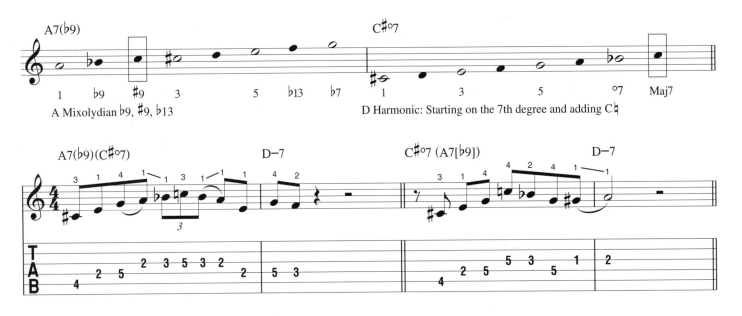

Fig. 8.14. Chord Scales and Melodic Phrases for A7(♭9) and C♯°7

♯II°7 = V7(♭9,♯9)/III

In addition to ♯I°7, other diminished 7th chords can be analyzed as secondary dominants. In the key of C major, D♯°7 is ♯II°7 and the upper structure of B7(♭9), V7(♭9)/III. By treating D♯°7 as B7(♭9), you can play an E harmonic-minor scale starting from the 7th degree. This scale is the same as B Mixolydian ♭9, ♯9, ♭13.

Fig. 8.15. E Harmonic Minor from the 7th Degree over D♯°7

The ♯II°7 is often used in the following progression: IMaj / ♯I°7 / II–7 / ♯II°7 / III–7. It's commonly found in standard tunes, such as "Easy Living" and "Ain't Misbehavin'." The accompanying melodic example uses harmonic minor scales over both ♯I°7 and ♯II°7.

Track 59

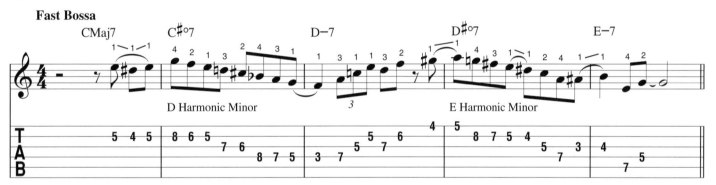

Fig. 8.16. Melodic Example Using Harmonic Minor Scales for ♯I°7 and ♯II°7

♭III°7

D♯°7 is enharmonically the same as E♭°7 (♭III°7). However, D♯°7 resolves upward by a half step to E–7 while E♭°7 usually resolves down by a half step to D–7.

The most common progression for ♭III°7 is III–7 / ♭III°7 / II–7, as in the second eight bars of Cole Porter's "All of You" (in the key of E♭ major): G–7 / G♭°7 / F–7 / B♭7.

The enharmonic spelling of D♯°7 and E♭°7 allows you to play an E harmonic minor scale over E♭°7, but it sounds different because E♭°7 resolves down one-half step to D–7, and this creates a deceptive resolution. When diminished 7th chords resolve in ascending motion, it's easy to hear their function as secondary dominants with expected resolution up a half step. Descending diminished 7th chords are trickier because their function as secondary dominants is disguised by the fact that they don't resolve in the expected manner. You also need to find different melodic resolutions when improvising over descending diminished chords.

Track 60

Figure 8.17 illustrates the use of harmonic minor scales for ♯I°7 and ♭III°7.

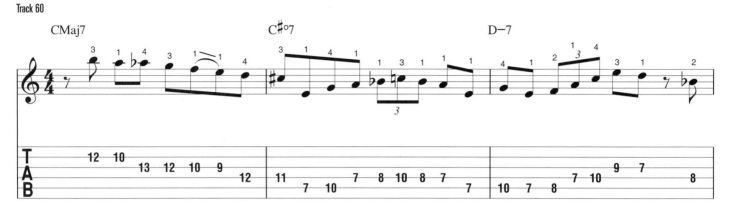

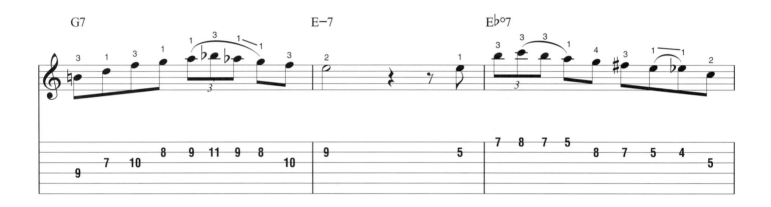

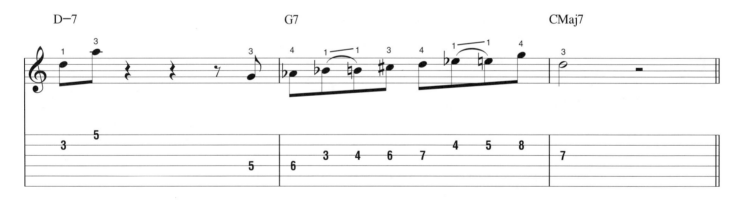

Fig. 8.17. *Melodic Examples Using Harmonic Minor Scales for ♯I°7 and ♭III°7*

I°7 and ♭III°7 = V7(♭9)/III

I°7 is enharmonically the same as ♭III°7. It is often found as a delayed resolution to IMaj7, as in the following progression: II–7 / V7 / I°7 / IMaj7. For I°7, you can play the same scale as for V7(♭9)/III; over C°7, play E harmonic minor.

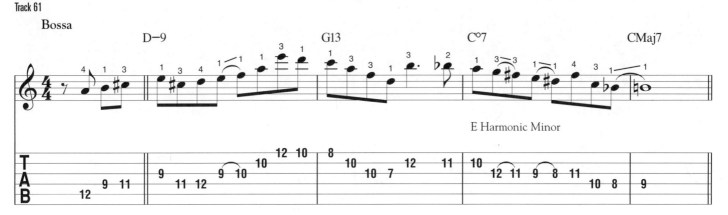

Fig. 8.18. *Melodic Example Using Harmonic Minor Scale over I°7 as V7(♭9) / III*

George Gershwin's "Embraceable You" uses a I°7 in measure 2, and the eighth measure of "I Wish I Knew" contains a tonic diminished 7th as a delayed resolution to IMaj7. Before Miles Davis reharmonized it, the first chord in "Stella by Starlight" was originally D♭°7, ♭III°7 in the key of B♭ major.

♯IV°7 = V7(♭9,♯9)/III

♯IV°7 is enharmonically ♯II°7 (or ♭III°7) and I°7, and uses the same harmonic-minor scale as V7(♭9)/III. Over F♯°7 in the key of C major, you can play an E harmonic minor scale.

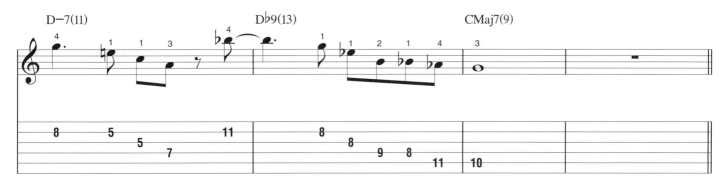

Fig. 8.19. *Melodic Example Using Harmonic Minor Scale over ♯IV°7 as V7(♭9)/III*

♯IV°7 = V7(♭9,♯9)/V

There is an alternative, more commonly used scale for ♯IV°7 when it functions as V7(♭9)/V. For example, F♯°7 is the same as D7(♭9), which is V7(♭9)/V in the key of C major. Figure 8.20 shows the 8-tone scale for ♯IV°7, along with an example of its use. Note that the major 7th has been added as an available tension on the diminished 7th chord.

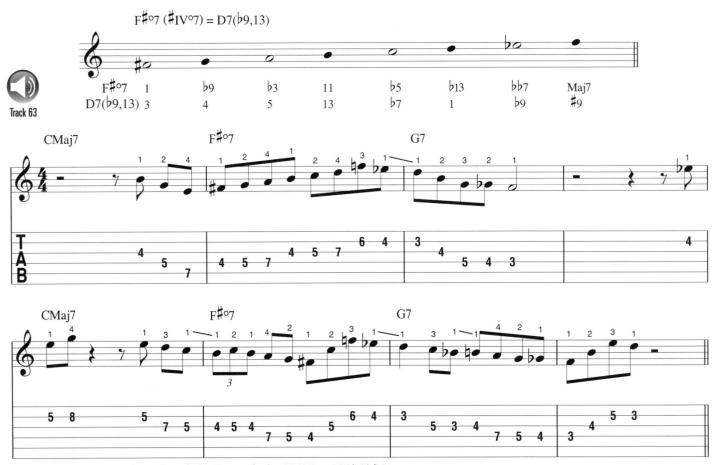

Fig. 8.20. 8-Note Scale and Melodic Example for ♯IV°7 as V7(♭9)/V

♯V°7

The ♯V°7 functions as V7(♭9)/VI. In the key of C major, G♯°7 sounds like E7(♭9) resolving to A–7 and takes an A harmonic-minor scale. It is found in "My One and Only Love," and its enharmonic equivalent, ♭VI°7, is in the second measure of Jobim's "Wave." Enharmonically, ♯V°7 is the same as II°7, IV°7, and VII°7 (IV°7 is found in the third measure of "The Nearness of You"). If you reduce these chords to enharmonic spellings of II°7, then any diminished 7th chord that can be analyzed as II°7 can take the same scale as V7/VI.

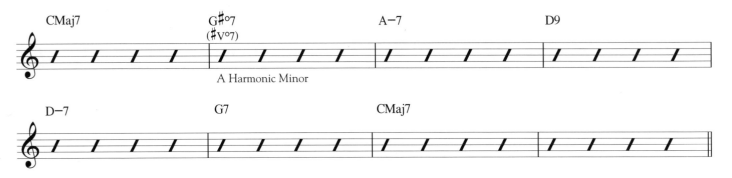

Fig. 8.21. Progression Using ♯V°7

Ascending Diminished 7th Chords That Function as Secondary Dominants

Use the following chart to help you memorize the ascending diminished 7th chords and corresponding scales you learned in this chapter.

A Mixolydian ♭9, ♯9, ♭13   D Harmonic Minor from the 7th degree (8-tone scale)

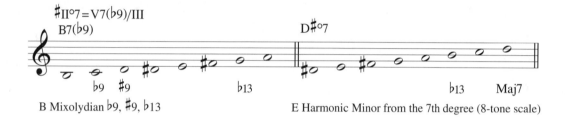

B Mixolydian ♭9, ♯9, ♭13   E Harmonic Minor from the 7th degree (8-tone scale)

D Mixolydian ♭9, ♯9, 13   G Harmonic Major from the 7th degree (8-tone scale)

E Mixolydian ♭9, ♯9, ♭13   A Harmonic Minor from the 7th degree (8-tone scale)

Fig. 8.22. Ascending Diminished 7th Chords with Secondary Dominant Function

Descending Diminished 7th Chords

Although the dominant function is disguised, descending diminished 7th chords can be analyzed as secondary dominants.

    I°7 and ♭III°7 can be analyzed as V7(♭9)/III
    ♭VI°7 can be analyzed as V7(♭9)/VI

Progressions Using Diminished 7th Chords

These common progressions use diminished 7th chords and are examples from standard jazz tunes quoted in this chapter.

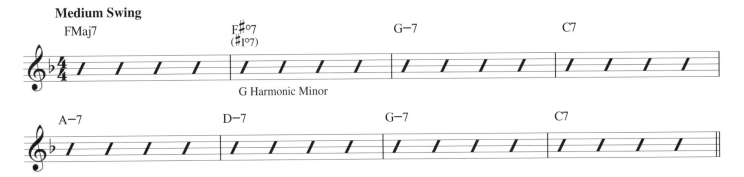

Fig. 8.23. *"Do You Know Miss Jones?" Progression Using ♯I°7*

Here is an example of a progression that uses both ♯I°7 and ♯II°7 in the key of F major.

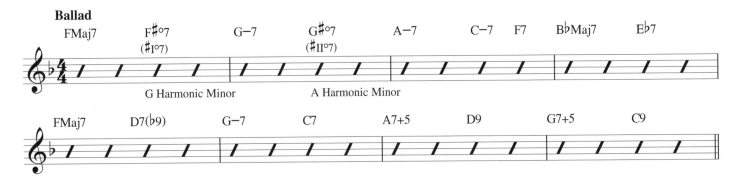

Fig. 8.24. *"Living Easy" Progression Using ♯I°7 and ♯II°7*

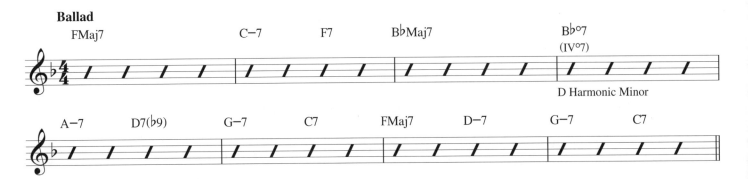

Fig. 8.25. *"Nearly You" Progression Using IV°7*

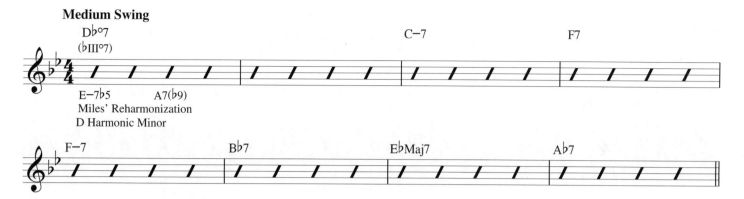

Fig. 8.26. *"Stella and the Starlight" Progression*

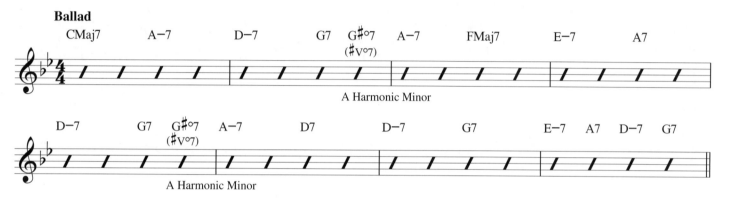

Fig. 8.27. *"My Only Love" Progression*

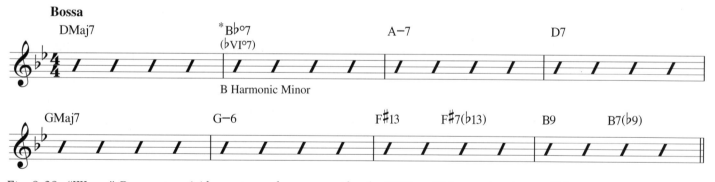

Fig. 8.28. *"Waves" Progression. *Alternative scales you can play for B♭°7 are D harmonic minor or D harmonic major, depending on whether you want to use F or F♯ as a passing tone.*

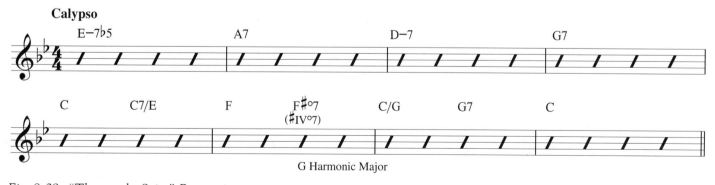

Fig. 8.29. *"Thomas the Saint" Progression*

Track 64

IF IT HAPPENED TO YOU

Fig. 8.30. *"If It Happened to You"* (Trio Track)

CHAPTER 9

The Symmetrical Diminished Scale

Another scale that is used to improvise over diminished 7th chords is the *symmetrical diminished scale*. It is composed of the chord tones and available tensions a whole step above each chord tone. The resulting scale has symmetrically alternating intervals: whole step, half step, whole step, half step, etc.

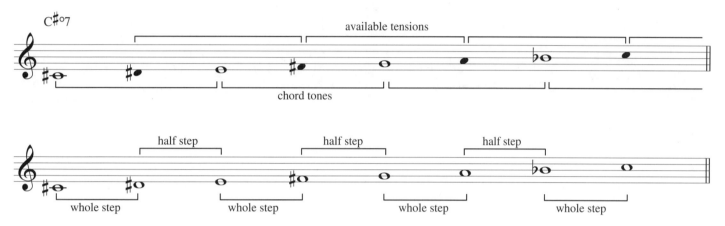

Fig. 9.1. *Symmetrical Diminished Scale*

In the same way that diminished 7th chords have four possible tonics, the symmetrical diminished scale has four possible names as well. The C♯ diminished scale is the same as the E, G, and B♭ diminished scales.

The symmetrical diminished scale works equally well over any diminished 7th chord regardless of its function in a key. It has a very different sound than the harmonic minor scale because the diminished scale contains passing tones that are non-diatonic to the relative key of the moment; therefore, it tends to sound more "outside."

Figure 9.2 is a comparison of the harmonic minor and symmetrical diminished scales and their passing tones for C♯°7 (♯I°7 in the key of C major). The D harmonic minor scale contains diatonic passing tones from the key of C major. The C♯ symmetrical diminished scale contains two non-diatonic passing tones (D♯ and F♯).

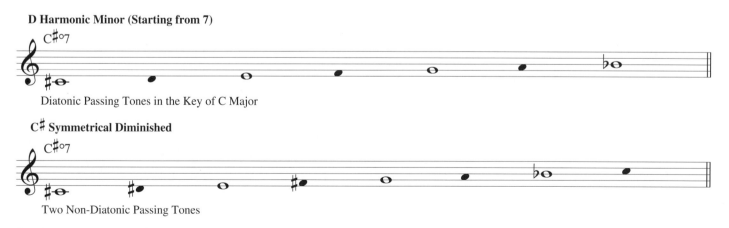

Fig. 9.2. *Comparison of Harmonic Minor and Symmetrical Diminished Scales*

You should experiment with the different sounds of these two scales by playing them over diminished 7th chords. The harmonic-minor scale sounds more "inside," while symmetrical diminished sounds more "outside."

Here are some melodic examples using the symmetrical diminished scale over #I°7 and ♭III°7 in the key of C major.

Track 65

Fig. 9.3. Solo Using the Symmetrical Diminished Scale over #I°7 and ♭III°7

Tensions from the symmetrical diminished scale can be used to approach each chord tone from a half step below.

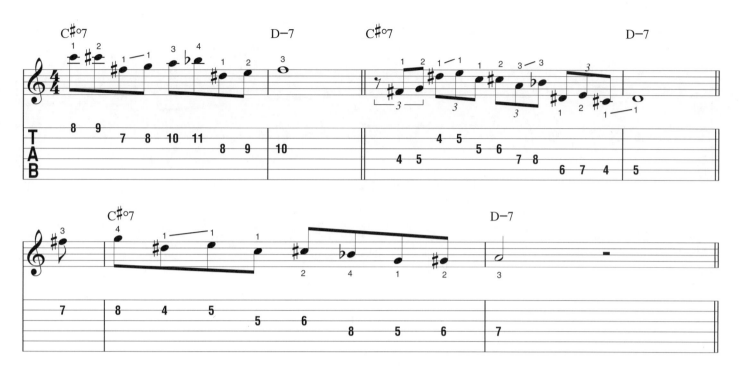

Fig. 9.4. *Approaching Chord Tones from a Half Step Below*

Playing the symmetrical diminished scale over a diminished 7th chord, the available tensions are a whole step above each chord tone and therefore spell another diminished 7th chord a whole step above the original chord. The tensions on C#°7 spell a D#°7 chord.

Fig. 9.5. *Tensions on Diminished Chords, One Whole Step above Each Chord Tone*

Track 66

The D♯°7 arpeggio can be used to create more complex lines for improvisation over C♯°7. Figure 9.6 contains examples of this approach where the notes of the D♯°7 arpeggio have been circled so that you can easily recognize them within the melodic phrases.

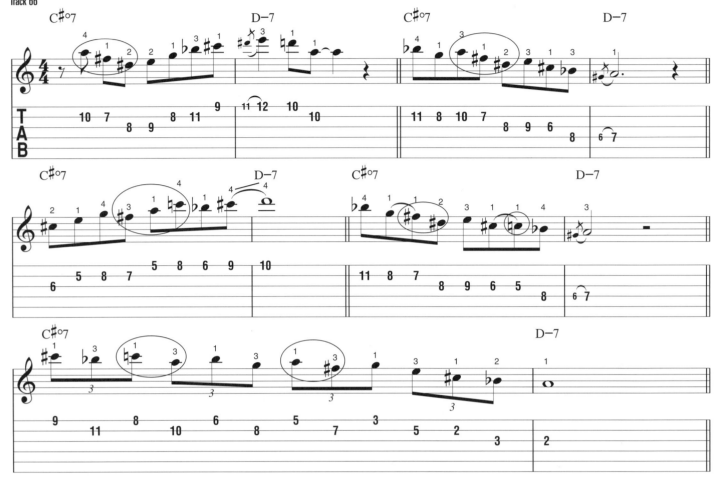

Fig. 9.6. Melodic Examples of D♯°7 Arpeggio over C♯°7

Track 67

Melodic patterns from the symmetrical diminished scale can be moved up or down the fretboard by intervals of minor thirds. Figure 9.7 shows some melodic pattern for C♯°7 moved up in minor third intervals, resolving to different degrees of D–7. The basic fingering remains similar as you move up the fretboard.

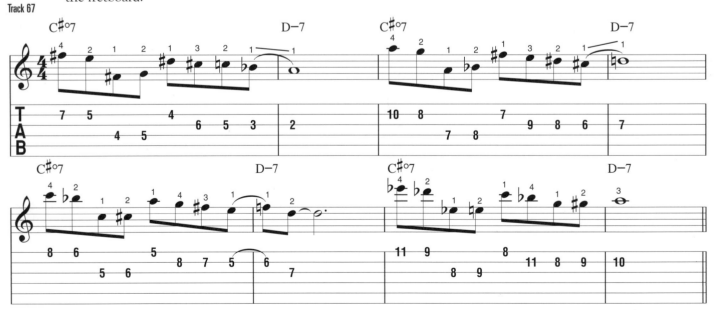

Fig. 9.7. Moving C♯°7 Pattern up the Fretboard

CHAPTER 10

The Four Tonic System

With four possible tonics in a diminished 7th chord, each chord degree can be lowered a half step to produce four separate dominant 7th chords from any one diminished 7th chord, hence the term "four tonic system." These four dominants can in turn be used as substitutes for each other to create a more complex and rich palette of sounds for improvising over standard progressions, and especially over V7 chords.

For example, an F°7 chord (F, A♭, C♭, D) produces dominant 7th chords E7, G7, B♭7, and D♭7. Beware of enharmonic spellings.

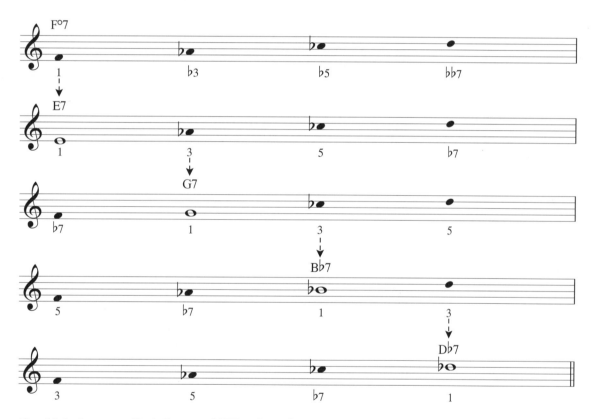

Fig. 10.1. Lowering Each Degree of F°7 to Reveal Four Dominant Chords E7, G7, B♭7, D♭7

A symmetrical-diminished scale can be played starting a half step above the root of any dominant 7th chord. Figure 10.2 is an example of an F diminished scale played over an E7 chord. The available tensions on E7 are ♭9, ♯9, ♯11, and 13. Again, beware of enharmonic spellings.

Fig. 10.2. F Diminished Scale One Half Step above E7

Track 68

There are several possible fingerings for diminished scales. Here is a fingering for the F diminished scale starting on E on the 5th string. Try playing this over E7(♭9), E7(♯9), or E7(♭9,13).

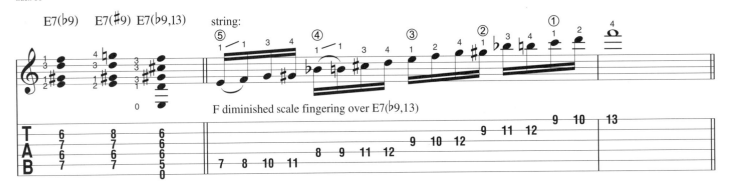

Fig. 10.3. Fingering for F Diminished Scale

The F diminished scale can be played over all four dominant chords derived from the F°7 chord: E7, G7, B♭7, and D♭7, resulting in a four tonic system that contains tensions ♭9, ♯9, ♯11, and 13 of all four dominant 7th chords.

Fig. 10.4. F Diminished Scale over Four Dominant Chords Derived from F°7

Improvising over Dominant 7th Chords Using Diminished Major 7th Arpeggios

To avoid a purely symmetrical sound when playing a diminished 7th arpeggio, build a diminished triad with a major 7th starting on each degree of the diminished 7th chord. This way, you'll get four separate arpeggios. The unusual sound of these arpeggios allows for more creative options when improvising over the four related dominant 7th chords.

Note: the fingering in figure 10.5 is shown in one position, but all four arpeggios can be transposed up or down by intervals of minor thirds and remain in the same key while covering all the areas of the fretboard.

These four diminished (Maj7) arpeggios can be played over E7, G7, B♭7, D♭7.

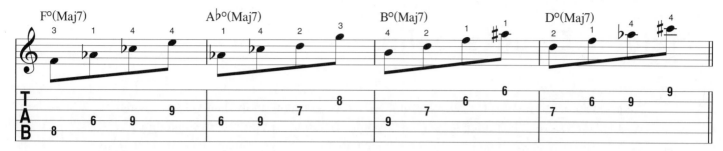

Fig. 10.5. Diminished (Maj7) Arpeggio Fingerings

The next step is to create melodic phrases with these arpeggios and play them using different melodic resolutions to the intended tonic of each dominant 7th chord.

Track 69

For example: E7 resolves to AMaj7, G7 resolves to CMaj7, B♭7 resolves to E♭Maj7, and D♭7 resolves to G♭Maj7. These lines will use various combinations of melodic extensions (♭9, ♯9, ♯11, and 13).

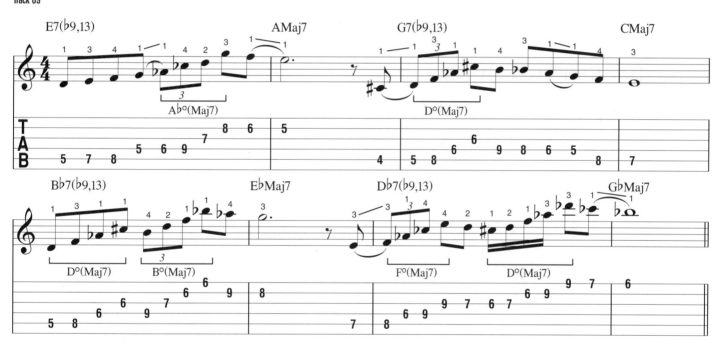

Fig. 10.6. Melodic Phrases Using Diminished (Maj7) Arpeggios

The advantage of this four-tonic system is that the same lines will work over different chords. For example, the last two lines of figure 10.7 (B♭7 to E♭Maj7 and D♭7 to G♭Maj7) can also be played over G7 to CMaj7 and B♭7 to E♭Maj7 respectively. The lines stay the same, but the harmony has changed.

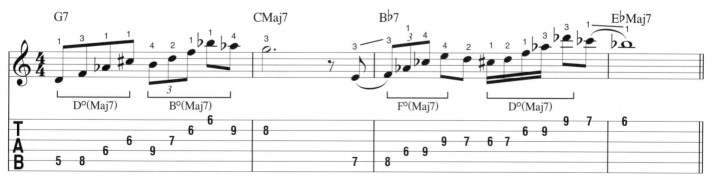

Fig. 10.7. The Same Lines over Different Chords

CHAPTER 11

Melodic Counterpoint

Traditional counterpoint is the relationship between two or more individual voices moving in varied directions. The principles of counterpoint play an important role in single-line improvisation, creating the impression of two separate voices interacting with each other. This contrapuntal effect is called "melodic counterpoint" or "compound lines."

In this chapter, you will learn the elements of melodic counterpoint by playing comparative examples from J. S. Bach, Charlie Parker, and other renowned jazz musicians.

In order to understand how compound lines work, let's examine the principles of counterpoint that define the directional movement between individual melodic lines or voices.

The three basic types of melodic motion are parallel, contrary, and oblique.

Parallel Motion

Parallel motion is the movement of two melodies in the same direction, either ascending or descending.

Fig. 11.1. Parallel Motion

Also called "similar motion," the intervals between the lines don't have to precisely match in order to be considered parallel.

Figure 11.2 is an example from Bach's *Violin Partita No. 1 in B Minor* of three separate lines moving in descending parallel motion. In this section, you can hear the voice leading of open position triads, B–, A, and G.

Track 70

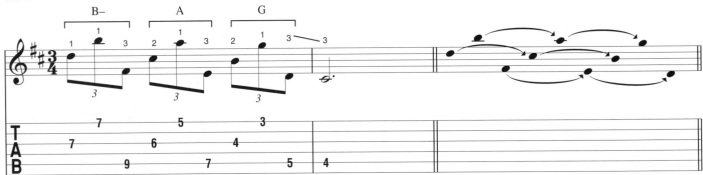

Fig. 11.2. Parallel Motion in Bach

A similar approach in the style of Charlie Parker features two parallel lines on B♭ rhythm changes. In jazz, compound lines don't necessarily outline the harmonic progression, since they are usually played on top of a bass line or chordal accompaniment.

Track 71

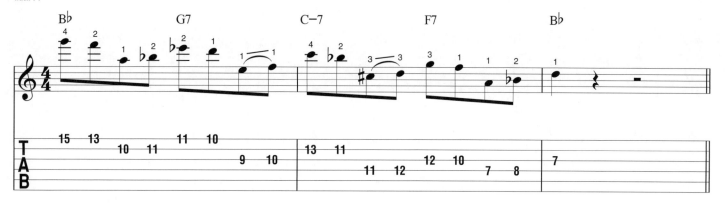

Fig. 11.3. Parallel Motion in Jazz

Here is the same example with the two lines indicated by note stems in opposite directions. The brilliant part of this phrase is that it's simply two B♭ major triads in parallel motion. (See the circled notes that identify the triads.) The top line descends diatonically, while the bottom line contains chromatic approaches from below the triad chord tones. This type of dual approach is referred to as "diatonic from above, chromatic from below."

Fig. 11.4. Diatonic from Above, Chromatic from Below

Track 72

Here is an example in the style of Jim Hall: A three-note motif composed of parallel octaves with a fifth tucked in between, it's the rhythm that makes this line sound interesting.

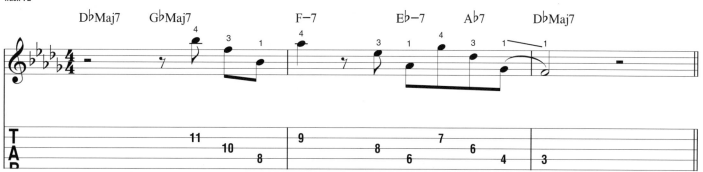

Fig. 11.5. Parallel Octave Example in the Style of Jim Hall

Another example in the style of Jim Hall, figure 11.6 has two lines that descend in parallel motion. In measure 3, the G melodic-minor scale over G–7 brightens up the sound and sustains the intervallic continuity.

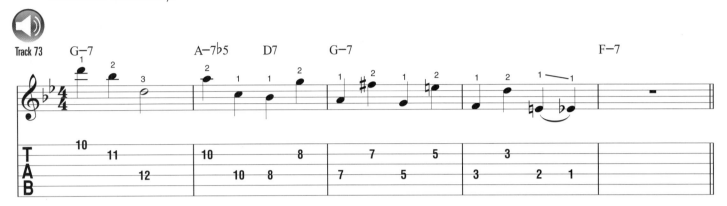

Fig. 11.6. Similar Motion

Figure 11.17 uses parallel fifths and syncopated rhythm to outline a I / VI / II / V progression in D♭ major.

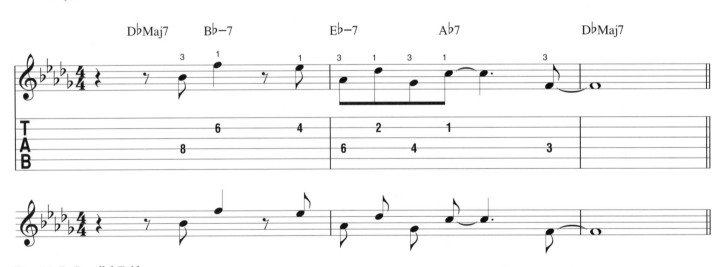

Fig. 11.7. Parallel Fifths

Figure 11.8 is an example of parallel G minor-pentatonic scales descending over a C–7 chord. Other rhythmic combinations work with the same notes.

Fig. 11.8. Parallel G Minor-Pentatonic Scales

Rhythmic displacement is a valuable technique to develop parallel lines. Figure 11.9 is an F melodic-minor scale played over B♭7(♯11,13).

Fig. 11.9. Rhythmic Displacement

Parallel lines in figure 11.10 capture the harmonic resolutions in a II–7♭5 / V7(♭9) / I– progression in D minor.

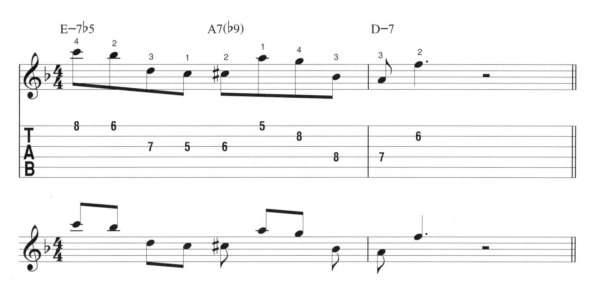

Fig. 11.10. Parallel Lines

This last example is a spectacular section from Bach's *Violin Partita No. 1 in B Minor* with three separate voices descending in parallel motion.

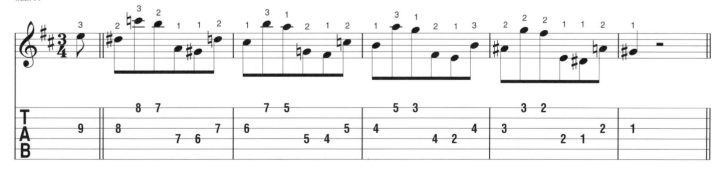

Fig. 11.11. Bach's Violin Partita No. 1 in B Minor

Contrary Motion

Contrary motion is the movement of two melodies in opposite directions. For example, if the top line moves up, the bottom line moves down (expansion), or more commonly, when the top line moves down, the bottom line moves up (contraction), as the two lines converge on a single target note.

The two types of contrary motion:

Fig. 11.12. Contrary Motion

The following example of contrary motion is presented first as a single line over a C– chord. A closer look reveals two separate voices moving in opposite directions (contraction) and converging on the target note, C. The top line is a descending C minor scale, while the bottom line implies a dominant approach: G7 to C–.

Fig. 11.13. Contrary Motion

Adding chromatic notes is common in jazz and often used in combination with compound lines to produce more complex melodies.

In figure 11.14, the top line descends in a scale-like manner while the bottom line ascends with chromatic approaches to the target notes. In figure 11.15, the individual lines are indicated with stems in opposite directions and the target notes are circled.

Fig. 11.14. "All the Things You Are"

Fig. 11.15. "All the Things You Are" Contrary Motion Analysis

Charlie Parker used contrary motion to create serpentine lines that weave in and out like an Italian sports car on the Amalfi coast. Figure 11.16 includes octave displacement (another technique inherited from J. S. Bach) between the notes B and A♭ in the first measure. Figure 11.17 is a melodic analysis with stems in opposite directions to illustrate the individual lines and the target note is circled.

Track 79

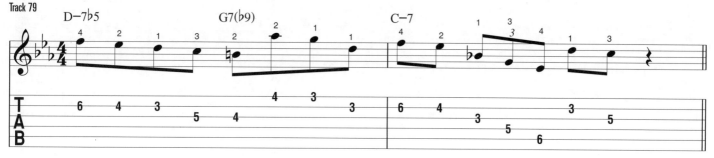

Fig. 11.16. Parker-Style Line with Contrary Motion

Fig. 11.17. Charlie Parker: Analysis of Contrary Motion with Target Note

Figure 11.18 is another example in this style over a II–7(♭5) / V7(♭9) / I–7 in the key of B♭ minor.

Track 80

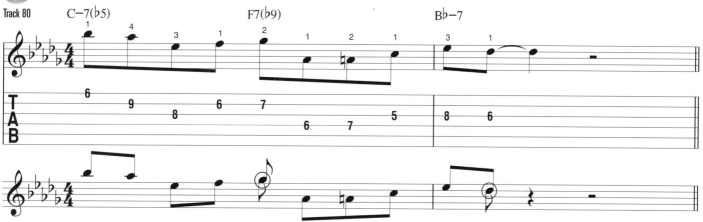

Fig. 11.18. Contrary Motion over II–7♭5 / V7(♭9) / I–7

Contrary motion with two lines moving away from each other (expansion) is more exotic and rare, but beautiful when encountered.

Here is an example from J. S. Bach:

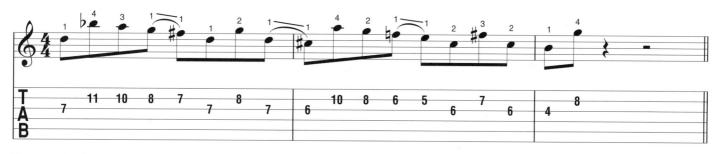

Fig. 11.19. Contrary Motion (Bach)

An example from "Bourrée' I," of Bach's *Cello Suite III*, shows just how expansive the intervals can become in this type of contrary motion. Starting with oblique motion in measure 5, the interval of a 5th (B down to E) expands towards the interval of a major 10th (C up to E) in measure 7.

Bourrée I Cello Suite III

Fig. 11.20. Bach's "Bourée I"

Figure 11.21 is an example of melodic expansion in the style of Charlie Parker.

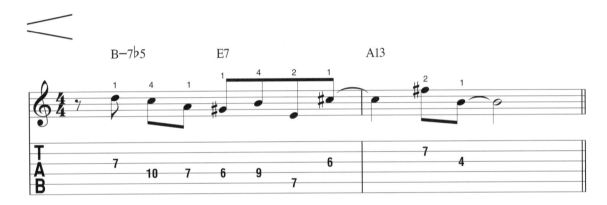

Fig. 11.21. Jazz Contrary Motion

Expanding contrary motion is less common because the intervals grow wider quickly, as you'll see in figure 11.22.

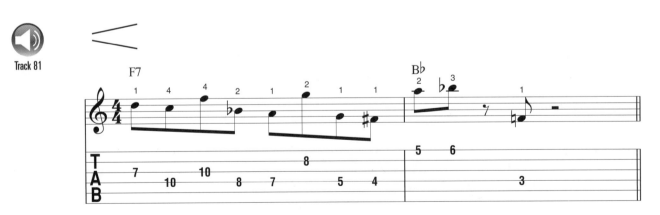

Track 81

Fig. 11.22. Contrary Motion with Expanding Intervals

Expansion can be used to add tensions to V7 altered chords in a typical II–7 / V7 / I / VI progression.

Fig. 11.23. Contrary Motion

Oblique Motion

Oblique motion is the movement of one melodic line in contrast to another that remains static by repeating the same pitch. Either the top or the bottom line can remain constant, sounding like a pedal point, while the other line moves in contrary motion, either ascending or descending.

There are four types of oblique motion:

Fig. 11.24. Oblique Motion

Bach's *Violin Sonatas and Partitas* contain numerous examples of oblique motion. In his "Bourée" from *Partita No. 2*, the top line stays on E while the lower line descends chromatically.

Fig. 11.25. Oblique Motion in Bach's "Bourée"

This classic Baroque cadence uses the tonic (D) in the upper voice, creating a suspension over the dominant chord (A), while the lower line descends.

Fig. 11.26. Oblique Motion in Cadence

An excerpt from Bach's "Courante," *Cello Suite II*, contains oblique motion both descending and ascending in measure 2, parallel motion with intervals of major and minor 6ths in measure 4, and oblique motion in measures 5 through 8.

Fig. 11.27. Example of Oblique Motion from Bach's "Courante," Cello Suite II

In a classic Charlie Parker approach to oblique motion, this II–7 / V7 / IMaj7 progression in F major uses the dominant pedal (C) on top while a chromatic line (G, G♯, A) moves upwards against it.

Track 83

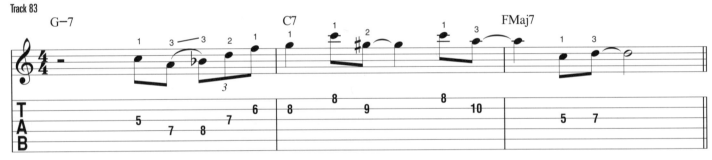

Fig. 11.28. Oblique Motion in the Style of Charlie Parker

Saxophonist Sonny Rollins combines oblique motion with a minimalist intervallic approach. Here is a progression in C major where the top line is the dominant pedal (G) and the bottom line moves in oblique motion. Once more, rhythm is an important factor.

Track 84

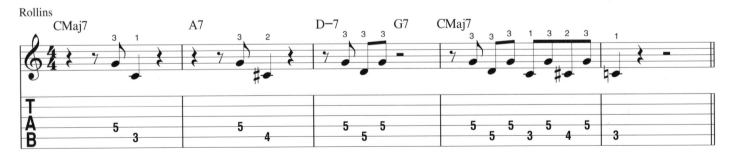

Fig. 11.29. Oblique Motion in the Style of Sonny Rollins

Another beautiful example of oblique motion, this one is from a Bach cello suite where the top line remains constant and the bottom line descends.

Fig. 11.30. Oblique Motion in Bach Cello Suite

Saxophonist John Coltrane used oblique motion to create melodic movement over static harmony such as major 7 chords, especially on ballads where time is stretched out farther. In figure 11.31, the pedal is on the bottom while the top line moves upwards.

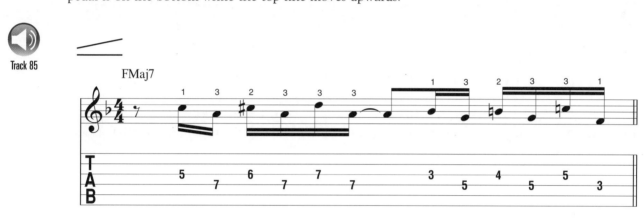

Fig. 11.31. Oblique Motion in the Style of John Coltrane

In similar Coltrane style, over D–7 / G7, the D remains constant on the bottom while the top line (F, G, G♯, A) moves upwards in oblique motion.

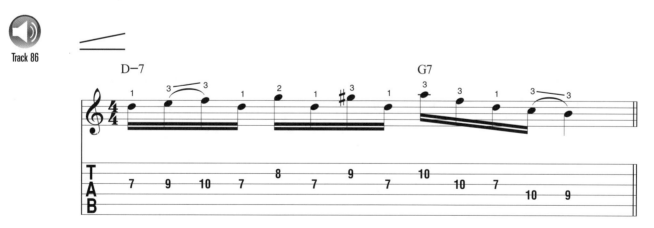

Fig. 11.32. Oblique Motion Coltrane Style over a D Pedal

A descending minor line cliché (figure 3.9) is part of the standard bebop approach to stretching the harmony on a II–7 / V7 progression. In this example of oblique motion, the D minor line cliché (D, C♯, C, B) descends against the chords while the top note, A, is heard as the pedal. The notes in the line cliché are circled.

Track 87

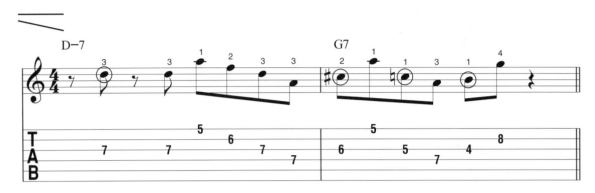

Fig. 11.33. Oblique Motion in Minor Line Cliché

Figure 11.34 is an example in the style of guitarist Grant Green, with the pedal (A) on the bottom and the line cliché descending above it.

Track 88

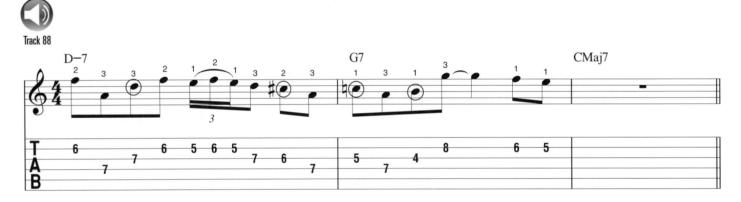

Fig. 11.34. Oblique Motion in Minor Line Cliché

In the style of Wes Montgomery, the minor line cliché becomes displaced, accenting the note C♯ on the downbeat of the second measure in figure 11.35.

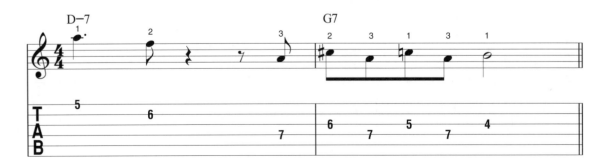

Fig. 11.35. Line Cliché in the Style of Wes Montgomery

And a "Parkeresque" take on this line might sound something like this:

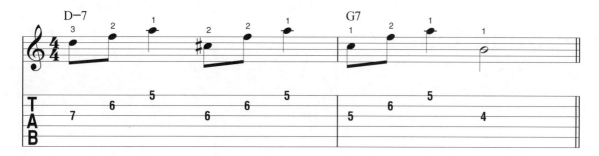

Fig. 11.36. Embellishment of Minor Line Cliché over II–7 / V7

Lastly, figure 11.37 is a line that uses a reverse rest stroke in the right hand picking—very useful for playing fast tempos!

Track 89

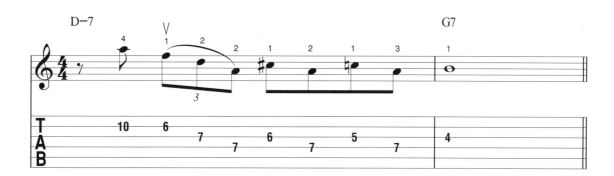

Fig. 11.37. Oblique Motion with Reverse Rest Stroke

A lot of examples were included in this chapter—so many, that it's difficult to improvise with all of them. The important point is to unlock your own creativity by exploring different resources.

Listening is an important part of studying contrapuntal motion: Bach's unaccompanied cello and violin suites and Charlie Parker's solos are essential. Get a copy of Charlie Parker's *Omnibook* (published by Criterion Music Corporation, distributed by Hal Leonard Corporation), and go through it with the original recordings to identify phrases that appeal to you. Once your ears unlock the secrets of parallel, contrary, and oblique motion, your fingers will find the notes more naturally on the fretboard.

There is a wide variety of individual artistic expression with which the ideas in this chapter can be interpreted—by you!

CHAPTER 12

Building a Solo: Chromatic Motion and Compound Lines

This chapter is an extension of ideas presented in chapter 11, with emphasis on the use of chromatic motion and compound lines. Beyond the examples of individual artistic expression that were demonstrated in the previous chapter, it's possible to distill these approaches into simplified form and use them to improvise.

Playing Horizontal Lines through Chord Changes

By playing horizontal lines through chord changes, you are no longer thinking vertically over a single chord. The ability to hear lines that develop melodic contour over longer spaces in time sustains interest for both the player and listener.

Looking at the microcosm of each harmonic situation and exploring the possibilities of which scales, arpeggios, or substitutions to play, it might be easy to assume that the intended approach is for an improviser to think of what to play on every chord, but that would misinterpret the real meaning behind knowing scales and the interconnectedness of harmony.

A more musical approach is to extract melodic material from within the scales by finding interesting shapes or intervallic motifs and transforming them through improvisation.

Parallel Descending Motion

The following is an example of parallel descending lines moving through a II / V / I / VI progression. Those famous parallel fifths that were avoided in species counterpoint have great value to a jazz improviser.

This approach explores the sound of chromatic alterations on dominant 7th chords by moving in chromatic or stepwise motion through the harmony. These alterations create a darker sound with more tension and resolution.

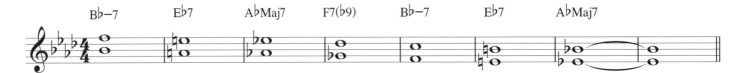

Fig. 12.1. Parallel Descending Lines

A simple contrapuntal melody (a compound line) can be formed from the previous study of parallel descending fifths. In figure 12.2, rhythm is an important element that makes parallel lines sound more musical.

Fig. 12.2. *Compound Line Using Descending Parallel Fifths*

Parallel Ascending Motion

Parallel ascending motion is another option. Figure 12.3 starts with the interval of a perfect fifth and moves upward in parallel motion.

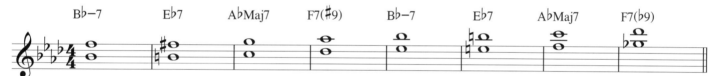

Fig. 12.3. *Ascending Parallel Fifths*

Using parallel ascending motion to build a melody, other notes can be added to embellish the lines while keeping the parallel motion intact. Rhythm is a key factor that makes the lines, as simple as they are, sound interesting.

Fig. 12.4. *Compound Line Using Ascending Parallel Fifths*

Contrary Motion

Contrary motion in an improvised melody disguises the roots of the progression by moving in the opposite direction.

Track 92

The following examples demonstrate contrary motion using two notes to create separate lines. These lines can then be embellished to develop more complex improvisation.

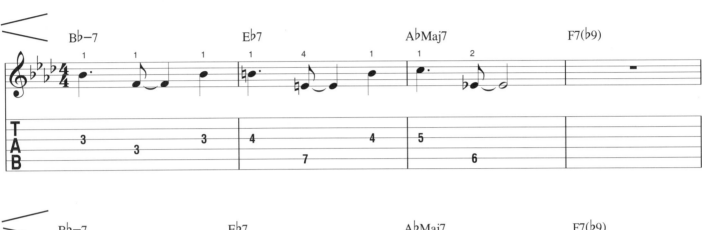

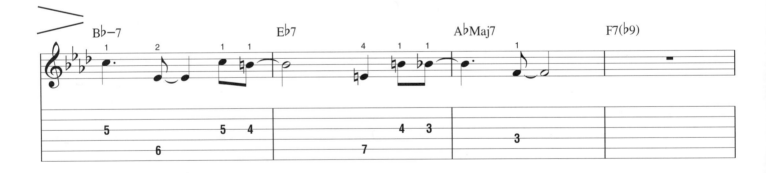

Fig. 12.5. Solo Using Contrary Motion

In the previous chapter, you learned that expanding contrary motion (where the intervals move apart in opposite directions) is rare because the intervals grow increasingly larger as the phrase grows longer. However the separation of the individual lines in this type of motion adds an interesting dimension to improvised melodies.

Figure 12.6 is an example of an expanding phrase that begins with an octave, increasing to an interval of a twelfth in measure 4 (D♭ up to A♭). Measures 5 and 6 have contracting intervals in contrary motion.

Track 93

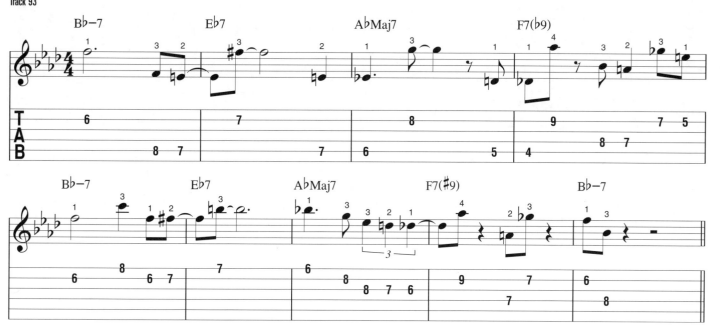

Fig. 12.6. Expanding Phrase with Contrary Motion

Creating separation and clarity between individual lines can be challenging, but with practice, it's possible to sound as if two improvisers are playing "call and response" in two distinct registers of the guitar.

One way to accomplish this is to alternate lines between odd and even numbered strings while maintaining an equal distance of one string between the two voices.

For example, strings 1 and 3 or strings 2 and 4. If you play a line on the 1st string, the second line is played on the 3rd string. Once the top line moves to the 2nd string, then the response is on the 4th string, and if the top line is played on the 3rd string, the second line is on the 5th string. Figure 12.7 is an example of this approach.

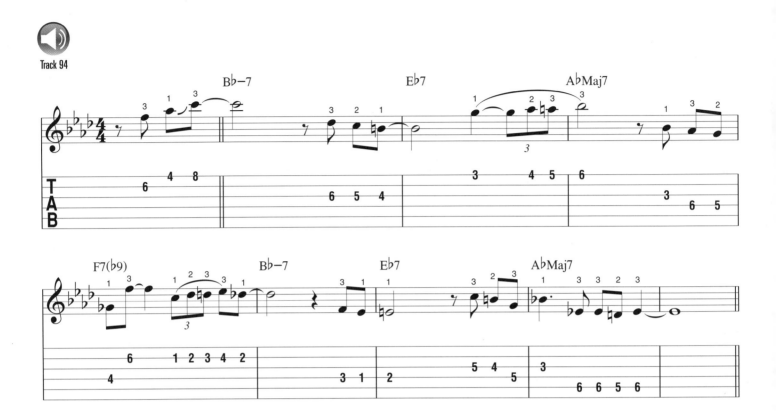

Track 94

Fig. 12.7. Call and Response Using Alternating Strings

There are other ways to simplify the conceptual approach to spontaneous improvisation and develop melodic variations from basic minor triads.

- Substitute a minor line over a familiar progression.

- Play a minor triad one half step above the root of a dominant 7th chord.

- Use your ear to find resolutions. Listen for, and anticipate a note in the next chord where you can resolve the line.

- Choose three notes, and base a solo from that one idea.

- Using similar shapes and intervals, develop a solo by transposing through the harmony.

Figure 12.8 demonstrates two forms of a minor line—a minor triad with an added 9th. These lines can be played over a familiar II / V / I / VI progression.

First, learn two forms of these fingerings for each chord. There are very slight differences in the fingerings due to the positions on the neck, but for the most part, these two basic minor forms can be used to play across the entire range of the fretboard. The chords in parenthesis indicate which minor line is being played as a substitute over the original chord.

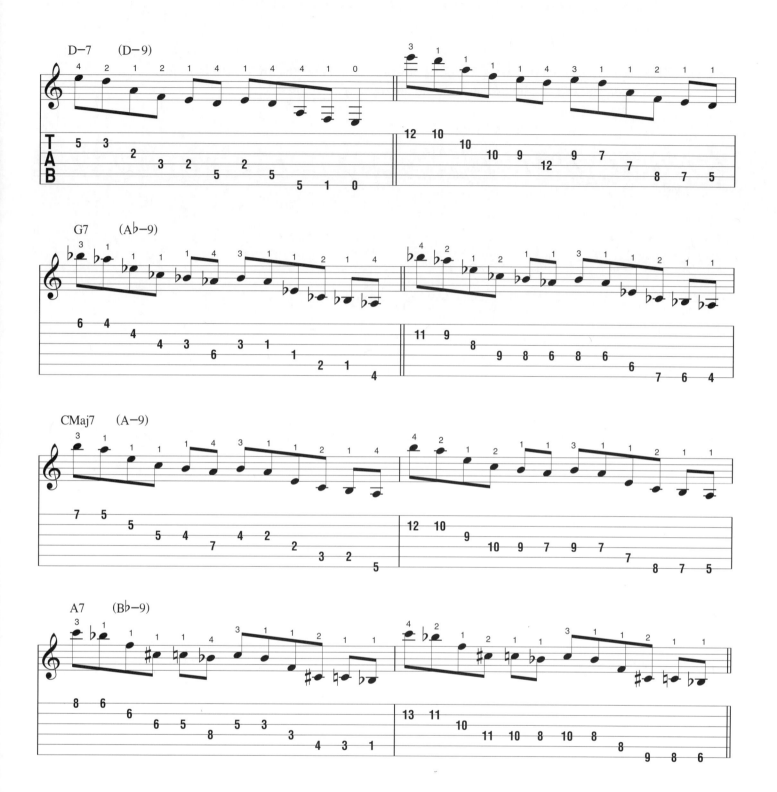

Fig. 12.8. Two Forms of Minor Line over a II / V / I / VI Progression

Playing minor line substitutions will lead you to new ideas for soloing over this progression.

Figure 12.9 shows the original II / V / I / VI progression and underneath is the minor line substitution you will be thinking about while improvising.

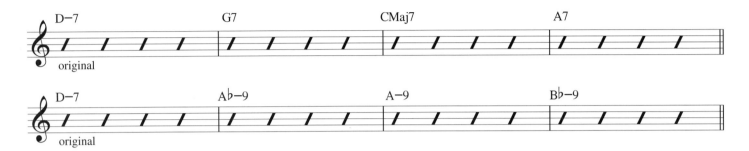

Fig. 12.9. Progression with Minor Line Substitution Used for Improvising

Figure 12.10 is a melodic example using the above minor line forms.

Track 95

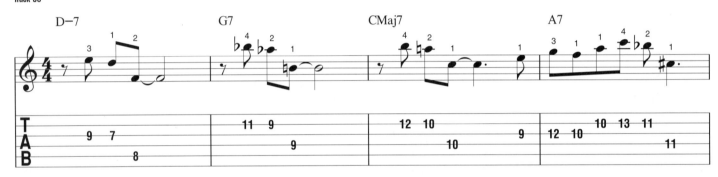

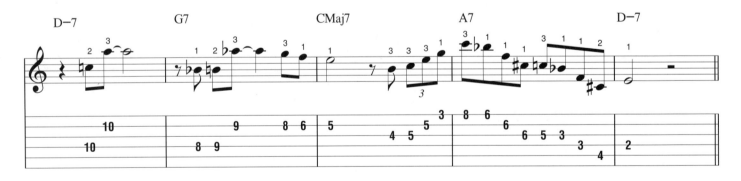

Fig. 12.10. Solo Using Minor Line Substitution

Tips for Developing Melodies

- Contrapuntal motion can be used sparingly, but with the effect of adding cohesiveness to a solo.

- Contrary motion in the melody disguises the root motion of the progression.

- By using *horizontal connections*, you are no longer thinking vertically over one chord, but are trying to connect horizontal lines through the changes.

- Extract melodic material from within the scales by finding motifs or interesting melodic shapes and intervals.

- The larger the interval in the motif, the more interesting it sounds.

- Choose three notes and base a solo from that by transposing through the harmonic sequence.

- Simplify: Use a basic concept and develop variations to create spontaneous improvisation—for example, a minor triad with a 9th.

- Use a minor line as a melodic substitution over a familiar progression.

- Look for the closest forms on the fretboard to connect between changes instead of jumping from one position to another.

- Use your ear to find resolutions. Listen for and anticipate a note in the next chord where you can resolve the melodic line.

- Play a minor triad one half step above the root of a dominant 7th chord to get the altered tensions.

- Work on developing lines that connect over longer harmonic distances and include several measures.

- Explore the sound of chromatic alterations on dominant 7th chords. It creates a darker sound with more possibilities for tension and resolution.

Author's Note

Jazz Improvisation and Melody

While the title of this book implies that harmony is the primary focus, my intent is always to integrate harmonic analysis and melodic invention. The sensation one feels when listening to a beautiful melody is unforgettable—possibly even more so than a great solo. Among my early influences, tenor saxophonist Ben Webster is an example of a great melodic player, and guitarist Charlie Christian was a very precise and passionate purveyor of melody. Expanding on Christian's approach, guitarist Jimmy Raney played seemingly effortless, fluid solos rich with contrapuntal melodies. Raney's duets with guitarist Attila Zoller exemplify the beauty of interactive contrapuntal improvisation. Pianist Bill Evans and guitarist Jim Hall recorded *Undercurrent* in 1959, setting the standard for melodic and rhythmic interplay, and opening my ears to the harmonic possibilities of this instrumental combination.

When I first heard tenor saxophonist Lester Young, I literally bought every one of his records I could find, and learned to sing many of his solos by ear. Lester's playing seems to float over the chord changes as he develops melodies at his own pace, independent of harmonic variations around him.

In recent years, I have gone beyond playing standards to concentrate more on spontaneous improvisation in recordings and performances. Sometimes called avant-garde or free jazz, the basics of good harmonic and melodic skills still apply, even when there are no chord changes to adhere to.

I hope you will have an opportunity to hear some of my recent compositions and recordings by visiting my Web site at www.garrisonfewell.com or www.myspace.com/garrisonfewell. If you have any questions or comments you would like to share, please feel free to drop me a line. I look forward to hearing from you!

Last Call: Bonus Track

I'd like to leave you with one more tune you can use to practice some of the ideas you have studied in this book: "Ocean's One." This tune is based on the changes to a famous standard and contains minor key harmony, secondary and non-diatonic dominants, and dominant substitution.

About the Author

Photo by Elio Buonocore

Guitarist Garrison Fewell has been a professor of guitar and ear training at Berklee College of Music for more than thirty years. He has taught at most major European Conservatories including Rotterdam, Maastricht, Graz, Cologne, Leipzig, Warsaw, the American School of Modern Music in Paris, and throughout the United States and South America. Garrison has conducted workshops for the International Association of Jazz Educators in New York City, Toronto, and the Montreux Jazz Festival, and taught harmony for the Polish Jazz Society, the New School, and Global Music Foundation.

With a mature, melodic sound and elegant, lyrical style of writing and playing, Garrison has established himself as a distinctive voice throughout his career. Critics have called him "one of today's most personal guitar players" (*Boston Phoenix*), "an assured stylist with a strong sense of tradition" (The New Yorker), "a player of virtuosity and swinging intensity" (UPI), and "refined, passionate, and inspiring" (*Guitar Player*). His diverse discography, beginning with 1993's Boston Music Award-winning "A Blue Deeper Than the Blue" (Accurate), counts multiple titles ranked on best of the year lists in publications such as *Coda*, *Guitar Player*, *Musica Jazz*, and his hometown *Philadelphia Inquirer*.

Garrison has performed and recorded with his quartet at New York City's Blue Note and Birdland jazz clubs, and international festivals such as Montreux, North Sea, Umbria, Clusone, Veneto Jazz, Copenhagen, Krakow, Budapest, Cape Verde, Africa, and Asuncion, Paraguay. His experience includes appearances with Tal Farlow, Benny Golson, Fred Hersch, Herbie Hancock, George Cables, Don Friedman, Jim McNeely, Hal Galper, Larry Coryell, Buster Williams, Cecil McBee, Cameron Brown, Steve LaSpina, Billy Hart, Kenny Wheeler, Tim Hagans, Dusko Goykovich, Cecil Bridgewater, Billy Harper, John Tchicai, Steve Swell, Roy Campbell, Jr., Khan Jamal, Norma Winstone, and Slide Hampton.

Garrison is the author of *Jazz Improvisation* (1984), *Jazz Improvisation for Guitar: A Melodic Approach* (Berklee Press 2005), *The Art of Harmony and Improvisation* (Carish 2007), and is a frequent contributor to *Guitar Player*, *Guitar Club*, and *Axe* magazines. He is the recipient of several major music grants: National Endowment for the Arts, Artslink, Arts International, and ACULSPEC.

More information is available at: www.garrisonfewell.com

Discography as Leader (or Co-Leader)

A Blue Deeper Than the Blue (Accurate, 1993). Garrison Fewell (guitar), Fred Hersch (piano), Cecil McBee (bass), Matt Wilson (drums).

Are You Afraid of the Dark? (Accurate, 1995). Garrison Fewell (guitar), Cecil McBee (bass), Matt Wilson (drums), Laszlo Gardony (piano).

Reflection of a Clear Moon (Accurate, 1997). Garrison Fewell (guitar), Laszlo Gardony (piano).

Birdland Sessions (Koch Jazz, 2000). Garrison Fewell (guitar), Jim McNeely (piano), Steve LaSpina (bass), Jeff Williams (drums).

City of Dreams (Splasch, 2001). Garrison Fewell (guitar), George Cables (piano), Steve LaSpina (bass), Jeff Williams (drums), Tino Tracanna (sax).

Red Door No. 11 (Splasch, 2003). Garrison Fewell (guitar), George Cables (piano), Attilio Zanchi (bass), Gianni Cazzola (drums).

Big Chief Dreaming (Soul Note, 2005). John Tchicai (tenor sax), Tino Tracanna (tenor and soprano sax), Paolino Dalla Porta (bass), Massimo Manzi (drums).

Good Night Songs (Boxholder, 2006). John Tchicai (tenor sax), Charlie Kohlhase (tenor, alto, bari sax), Garrison Fewell (guitar, percussion).

The Lady of Khartoum (Creative Nation Music, 2008). Garrison Fewell (guitar, percussion), Eric Hofbauer (guitar).

Variable Density Sound Orchestra (Creative Nation Music, 2009). Garrison Fewell (director, guitar, percussion), Roy Campbell, Jr. (trumpet), Achille Succi (alto sax, bass clarinet), Eric Hofbauer (guitar), John Voigt (bass), Miki Matsuki (drums), Alex Fewell (percussion).

One Long Minute (Nu Bop Records, 2009). John Tchicai (tenor sax and bass clarinet), Alex Weiss (alto and tenor sax), Garrison Fewell (guitar, bowed guitar, percussion), Dmitry Ishenko (bass), Ches Smith (drums).

Tribal Ghost at Birdland (Release pending). Garrison Fewell (guitar), John Tchicai (tenor sax), Charlie Kohlhase (tenor, alto, bari sax), Cecil McBee (bass), Billy Hart (drums).

Variable Density Sound Orchestra: Sound Particle 47 (Creative Nation Music, 2010). Garrison Fewell (guitar), Steve Swell (trombone), Roy Campbell, Jr. (trumpet), Achille Succi (alto sax, bass clarinet), Kelly Robereg (tenor sax), Eric Hofbauer (guitar), John Voigt (bass), Dmitry Ishenko (bass), Miki Matsuki (drums).

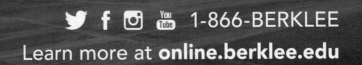
0316